Editorial

This editorial comes to you from Oaxaca, where I spent six weeks over Christmas and New Year among Mexican friends and relations. I spoke almost exclusively Spanish, at public occasions, in conversation, and found my English deprivation growing daily more acute. My ability to remember words (in conversations with myself, my only Anglophone companion) weakened. Wanting to use it in an email, I spent half an hour recovering the word 'superflux' from the tucks and folds of memory. My emails themselves became overlong, and my style reverted to that of the young Thomas Babington Macaulay. As a boy I loved Macaulay's elaborated sentences, the affectation yet vigour of his syntax, and his abundant vocabulary which wore its etymologies on its sleeve. *The History of England* was my Whiggish bible, and it took many years to recover from it. In the end Philip French, who produced some of my radio work, told me that my style was 'unspeakable' in at least one sense, perhaps two, at which point I began to write a less unnatural, a more sayable English.

In Oaxaca I also found that my Spanish, the first language in which I was fluent, has started to become uncertain. My vocabulary has lost so many words through disuse that every complex sentence becomes a series of inventive periphrases. I gave a long formal interview in Spanish, first in public at the University and then in private to a journalist, on my third day there. After that I started to lose my footing. I can't translate *between* my languages because each one speaks differently. When one acquires a new language, translation is natural, but when one inhabits two languages as a birthright the exercise is different. They are not interchangeable, there are no dependable equivalences and the approximations one achieves at some level falsify or compromise. One never quite says what one means in the first in the second, and vice versa.

Jorge Luis Borges suggests that forgetting Latin is part of one's knowledge of the language, a kind of inevitable refinement, like panning for gold where the dross is shed and only what memory regards as the pay dirt survives. Forgetting as a mode of learning. Older people have a lot of learning to get through. It's not unlike downsizing. You get to know which of your books really matter.

While I was in Mexico the ex-president of the United States Jimmy Carter died in Georgia at the age of a hundred. The *Guardian* (29 December) reported that this benign, kindly and evidently good man 'read the Bible in Spanish as part of his daily devotions'. In an interview he said,

> For more than forty years, my wife and I have read the Bible aloud every night. One night, she reads; the next night, I read. We go all the way through the Bible, then we go back and start over again. In the last fifteen or twenty years, we have read the Bible aloud in Spanish, just to practice our second language.

I've been musing on this form of spiritual activity. Carter knew the Bible well, from infancy, he had long chunks of scripture by heart, was a kind of Christian hafiz. In him religion was a renewable, creative force, whether he was teaching Sunday school or being commander in chief. At what age did he start reading the familiar words in Spanish, making them unfamiliar and new again, leavening his understanding?

I also wondered which translations he used. We know he received the New Marked Reference Bible in 1975 as a gift from his brother Billy. This may have been his Bible of preference, the King James (Authorised) Version of both Testaments with thematic colour coding, centre-column references, Bible readers 'Helps' with pictures and descriptions, 5,500 questions and answers on the scriptures, a full concordance and maps. The edition shapes and directs the way readers approach the text. It may be that the American Bible Society edition of the Bible in modern Spanish, *Dios Habla Hoy*, presented by visiting clergy to Mr Carter in 1980, his penultimate year in the White House, gave him a new purchase on the familiar texts, a new ear for what he knew by heart. It enhanced also his understanding of the many Americans with Spanish as their first language and their language of worship after the Second Vatican Council (1962–5). Some refer to his command of Spanish as 'rudimentary', yet sometimes teaching Sunday school (we are told) he would use the Spanish Bible, translating fluently into English as we went. *Dios Habla Hoy* is remarkably plain and direct, assuming this is the version he read. Moving between languages was a freedom he insisted on exercising. Aloud. It is a freedom that requires cultivation, it thrives on dialogue ('my wife and I') and can perish without it. It is easy to surrender it in a monoglot world. One can lose it without sensing the loss, until some trip into the past, among the now unfamiliar familiarities, brings the pain into focus. 'I can remember much forgetfulness', says Hart Crane. 'Forgetfulness is white.'

One moves eventually, inevitably, into the company of the old fools, straying between languages, finding and then losing meanings, bearings. Words. Philip Larkin's poem insinuates itself. Moving between lighted rooms, among people I almost recognise 'but can't quite name':

> each looms
> Like a deep loss restored, from known doors turning,
> Setting down a lamp, smiling from a stair, extracting
> A known book from the shelves; or sometimes only
> The rooms themselves, chairs and a fire burning…

It would seem that Jimmy Carter, who lived a hundred years, never took up lodging in that hotel.

Letters to the Editor

Catastrophic Doggerel

Robert Griffiths writes: Following my squib 'AI and Poetry' (*PNR* 276), I was interested to see Joey Connolly addressing some of the problems of computers 'writing poetry' in *PNR* 277 ('Todo'). He is right to lambast the Large Language Model (LLM) approach to this, which has recently excited so many. Pointing out that the need for these programs to train on massive volumes of text (thus inevitably sucking up the bad) sits uneasily with the relatively tiny volume of good poetry available, is on point. Like me, he was able to quote freely from the shit (what Connolly calls 'catastrophic doggerel') they consequently produce.

But even if these programs could train only on 'good' poetry, it is not clear how, in their production of what is statistically most likely in a word-string, they could produce anything original. It is not obvious that any analysis of the best poetry written before 1915 would have come up with the devastating third line of *Prufrock*. That line was not already waiting in that poetry; it was not even waiting in *language*. It arose from a particular human being's unique relationship to that poetry and the world. But perhaps the most serious problem for a poetry writing computer is that no one yet knows how poetry gets written. Writing good poetry is an expertise, but not even good poets, or good critics, know how to unpack this expertise. This is partly because a large element of this expertise is unconscious. Connolly notes that writing poetry requires 'intuition, empathy and musical sensibility to be attuned at the same time as our faculties of ratiocination'. But this admirable phrase still only hints at what is really going on. T.S. Eliot and Seamus Heaney have tried to articulate what all this involves, Eliot with his 'auditory imagination', Heaney with his talk of 'technique'. But both were merely gesturing at the unknown depths of human language production systems. It is there that part of the secret of poetry lies; it won't be found in language models. And even then, we won't account for what gave us the third line of *Prufrock*.

Trabs

Daniel James writes: I was about to write to congratulate all but some unknown one of the editorial team for the following from your submissions page, which I first took to be a world-beating example of how to combine the snide with the baroque:

'This year the June submission date has had to be postponed because one of the editors is undergoing eye operations (trabeculectomy) and will be out of commission.'

Trabs giving me 'beam', even a little one, I wondered what 'one of the editors' could have said. As it turns out, however, I wish them well!

The editors reply: The surgery on both eyes was a success and the editor in question is currently (and for weeks to come) gazing through the December submissions window.

News and Notes

Smoke Signals • *William Elliott, long-time friend and translator (with the late lamented Kazuo Kawamura, most recently of* New Selected Poems, *2015) of the Japanese poet Shuntarō Tanikawa, writes:* In the modern period of Japanese poetic volcanic eruptions, the latest was on 15 December 1931, at the birth of Tanikawa Shuntarō, poet. That eruption carried straight through 13 November 2024, when Tanikawa-san died in Tokyo at ninety-two of natural causes. He is survived by millions of readers. The kamikaze winds that once carried suicide pilots have continued blowing, sifting the poet's engaging ashes everywhere across Japan (and much of the globe). There will be no let-up in Tanikawa's presence. He remains a household word. Not incidentally, he is partially enurned in a Carcanet volume.

My poem 'Shun Remembered' was written in January 2020.

> You lived in a plague of words;
> spent decades swatting them away like gnats.
> Now we can answer your life-long question,
> 'Where do words come from?'
> They came, as they have always come,
> from 'that world' where you are now;
> that world of the eloquent silences
> that lay between the words of your poems.
> We are still stilled by those silences
> that you would say are the pulse of your poems.
> Words come. Words go. Your silences remain.

I wrote this elegy in advance, alert to the possibility that I might precede Shun in death or be otherwise incapacitated, in which case Nishihara-san would respectfully pass it along to Tanikawa Kensaku-san. The elegy 'Anoyo' was composed after the poet's death.

> Smoke rose in a pattern of puffs
> quickly read by the tribe across
> two creeks and the plain, a mile distant:
> *Return* – the order understood.
> An ill elder had now set out
> on his journey to the spirit world.
>
> The cursive hiragana text
> curling up from the distant stack
> read that Shuntarō had entered
> another phase of his journey
> on the narrow path to distant
> *anoyo*, where words yield to silence.

Kawamura-san died in 2015. Our colleague Nishihara Katsumasa took over and we continue translating. The translation of 'Shun Remembered' is by Nishihara Katsumasa.

(Shuntarō Tanikawa also composed the lyrics for the *Astro Boy* theme song and translated *Peanuts* into Japanese. His 1952 debut, *Two Billion Light Years of Solitude*, considered the cosmic in everyday life and was 'sensual, vivid but simple in its use of everyday language'. It preceded Márquez's *One Hundred Years of Solitude* and like it, though not on quite the same scale, became a bestseller. He translated *Mother Goose* and Maurice Sendak.)

Born To Be Wild • *New Zealand poet John Gallas remembers Fleur Adcock (1934–2024)*. Thursday 17 October. Sunny and warm. 2pm, a Requiem Mass for Fleur Adcock. Her street, one corner away from the church, is comfortably quiet. A large cheeseplant stretches over her upstairs window.

All Saints' Church, East Finchley. A full complement of friends, neighbours, acquaintances and admirers. In the vestibule, a screen-show of photos from Fleur's life: baby, teen and grandmother; Aotearoa/NZ and England; cigarettes, flares, parties, beaches, holidays, children, readings and honours.

The service is ritual, the content and music chosen by Fleur. Hymns, prayers, liturgy, psalms, homily, offertory, breaking of the bread, Communion and commendation.

Before the final prayers come the reflections and readings of family, friends, her publisher, academic-friends and a reading of 'Dragonfly': memories written by her sons, Greg and Andrew (read by wife and niece), Mia (niece), Sarah Duckworth, Marilyn Duckworth (read by Mia), praise and tales from Neil Astley, Janet Wilson, Julian Stannard, and lastly 'Dragonfly' (read by Lorraine Mariner).

The coffin, topped with religious and family items – a crucifix, a transistor radio – is carried away by Mia, Sarah and Angela: an image of bravery, family togetherness, mourning and pride that will remain, unforgettable, with all who were there.

Fleur was cremated at Islington Crematorium Chapel. On the way back to East Finchley tube station, I saw a van parking in the spot directly outside no.14 Lincoln Road: it was 'Bright Builders Ltd', and the radio inside was playing 'Born to Be Wild'.

Now time to read, or reread. Start with the three poems included in the first *Poetry Nation*: 'Richey', 'The Voyage Out' and 'Holiday Diaries, 1845 and 1971'. Knowing, of course, wonderfully, there are a few hundred more.

Old news is new news • The enigma of a lead coffin discovered beneath Notre-Dame may have been solved. The tenant of the sarcophagus could be the great French Renaissance poet Joachim du Bellay (died in 1560). Traditionally the occupant had been identified as 'the horseman'. The *Smithsonian Magazine* disclosed the discovery in September 2024. The sarcophagus, one of a pair, came to light in 2022. The other had the name of the dead man conveniently in an inscription. It was Antoine de la Porte, a priest who died aged eighty-three. Du Bellay was more reticent to disclose his identity but the magazine reports that 'Several compelling clues led the researchers to link the horseman to du Bellay. The poet's equestrian abilities are well documented: He once "rode from Paris to Rome, which is no mean feat when you have tuberculosis like he did," said a biological anthropologist at France's University of Toulouse III. "In fact, he almost died from it."' In *PN Review* 33, C.H. Sisson wrote about du Bellay and translated twenty sonnets from *The Regrets*. He quotes from Spenser's translations from the *Antiquitez*, noting that Spenser in *The Ruins of Rome* turned du Bellay's Italian into English sonnet form:

> Behold what wreake, what ruine, and what wast,
> And how that she, which with her mightie power
> Tam'd all the world, hath tam'd herselfe at last.
> The pray of time, which all things doth devouvre.

Oulipo loses a crucial syllable • Le Monde *reported*: Jacques Roubaud, the French poet and 'mathematician of words', and a key member of the Oulipo group from 1966 on, who was awarded the Prix Goncourt for poetry in 2021, died in December at the age of ninety-two years. He was a master of the poetics of wry restraint, a figure more approachable than many other Oulipo writers because of his sense of play with fixed form including the sonnet, the renga and the sestina. Strict forms require the most intense creative effort within language. One of the founders of Oulipo, Raymond Queneau, drew Roubaud into the centre of the group. He was an active translator from many languages – translation providing to the serious craftsman some of the strictest constraints and bringing into the host language compelling, not always familiar resources. His own formal inventions include the 'trident', the 'joséfine', the 'mongine' and other forms closely related to his first discipline, mathematics. One of the best ways into his work is the 2016 Gallimard 'anthologie personnelle', *Je suis un crabe ponctuel*, bringing together material from 1967 to 2014.

Nikki Giovanni • Also in December one of the key figures in American Black arts died, Nikki Giovanni. She was born in Knoxville, Tennessee, in 1943, and brought up in Cincinnati, Ohio. Yolande Cornelia 'Nikki' Giovanni grew up with other writers and artists affected deeply by the white terrorism that led to the murder of Emmett Till in 1955, the Montgomery bus boycott and the civil rights movement. In the six decades of her writing career she composed over fifty titles and miscellaneous works – poetry, essays, children's books. Her poetic career began with the self-published *Black Feeling, Black Talk* (1968), paid for by her grandmother. It was a success and led to her rise in literary and political fame. She went on to be a finalist in the National Book Awards and a poet laureate. Syreeta McFadden described her as 'a disruptor whose sensibilities as a writer were informed by her deep knowledge of history and the struggles of the civil rights and Black power eras. She used lyricism and poetry to capture the ups and downs of African American life in the late twentieth century, providing her students a blueprint to channel language, to dream, to shake up the world.'

Piedad Bonnett • In November Queen Sofia of Spain conferred her eponymous Iberoamerican award for poetry – the twenty-third – on the writer and dramatist Piedad Bonnett of Colombia. The presentation was made in the Hall of Columns at the royal palace in Madrid. Bonnett is widely celebrated in Latin America and has been translated into Dutch, French and other languages of Europe. One of her best-known works, from 2013, was her account of the illness and suicide of her son in *Lo que no tiene nombre*. In accepting the award, she ended her moving account of the necessity of poems, if not to change the world, then to broaden our sense of it and our abilities to respond to it. She ended with lines of verse in memory of her son who died thirteen years ago.

Reports

Water Poetics

ANTHONY VAHNI CAPILDEO

The city of York, a stately place of fortified walls and towers, and Roman remains instead of basements below Georgian terraced houses, nonetheless is familiar to those who live, work, or regularly visit, as a city of water. It is prone to flooding. With the increase in named storms hitting the UK, it is living its territorial precarity ever more closely. The University of York campus features bodies of water and is rich in waterfowl. One saintly runner duck and erstwhile social media star, Longboi, whose friendly towering guarded our wellbeing during the pandemic, has been commemorated by his own statue, and deserves an ode someday.

The writing of water in Old and Middle English texts is awesome and precise. As Carolyn Twomey and Daniel Anlezark note in *Meanings of Water in Early Medieval England* (2021), 'Water is fundamentally threatening to human beings even beyond the perils of too much and too little of it: metaphysically, water suggests a loss of self.' Yet water can be salvific, life-giving; it can reflect the fluency of wisdom, and image the powerful, unknowable divine. It is no surprise, then, that Water Poetics is one of the most exciting research strands at York, led by Dr Rebecca Drake, a medievalist by training and a poet in fact.

With the confluence of thought allowed by the circulation of people and texts, it was no surprise to me to find that Becca Drake's work, though originating elsewhere, aligns with Kamau Brathwaite's vision of tidalectics. For Brathwaite, the physical environment, its spiritual heritage, the shaping of history and sociopolitical forces currently at work are indivisibly part of the to-and-fro that is also language, also the layout of a poem on screen or page. Another image for Drake's process: imagine the branching, nerve-like structure of a fully opened historical dictionary entry for 'water'. The title 'Water Poetics' does not circumscribe a 'field'. It proceeds indeed like water. Individual and shared research practice might include observational time at Robin Hood's Bay, or with river-dredged artifacts in a museum. Water poetics is the study of writing about water, and it is the immersion of a page in water; speaker events in a university room, spoken word events on a boat... The body that is present at all these, and the glistening channels of the brain, collect up and distill the research findings.

Water poetics sends you on journeys inwards and outwards; inwards to aquatic memories, outwards to interdisciplinary encounters. For example, the 'natural navigation' that Tristan Gooley writes about in *How to Read Water: Clues, Signs, and Patterns from Puddles to the Sea* (2016). To enjoy his immediately practical yet profoundly traditional style of reading water – orientating oneself waterwards, you do not need to live near the coastline, or by a stream, or within reach of a tidal island (I live not far from all these). A spill on a table is enough water for you to begin reading – for the joy of knowledge, play, and survival. Not 're-enchantment'. Water on its own is 'enchanting' enough, especially in its ability to quench modern technological devices. The joy is more like the wonder of meeting, and deepening a relationship. *How to Read Water* is the kind of book to which I turn when not writing poems. It feels like being inside our world, the way I am inside language when writing a poem.

Every one of us could find the springs of our poetics if we chart our lived experience with a mind of water. Reading the sea for rip tides is a habit I acquired early and naturally, around the same time and in similar ways to reading 'dog ears' in the cloth of an unevenly hemmed dress. These readings did not feel like a skill being exercised, but something I reached into. They did not belong to different worlds. They were of the one world of always being on the fringe of other things that might mingle with you. The sense of being amidst patterns, both discernible and mysterious, other as well as close. Patterns that could raise themselves, sometimes overwhelmingly, into environments.

A quick, earthy smell might rise from the side of a precipice on Trinidad's north coast roads. Accompanying it, a low gurgling, an intense, almost intentional-seeming sound. Smell and sound on the verge of nourishment. I recognized its relative one English autumn, in the warble in the throat of an unseen fox at night that had made a good warm kill in a cold field. Similarly, those rain-fed Caribbean springs often remained invisible, not very big at all; though they might translate into waterfalls, or landslides. The ocean beyond the cliffs could be seen and not heard, while the spring might be heard and not seen. I like to believe that we are able to be reprogrammed; but early experience truly is a source for how we think throughout our lives, and what we are drawn to think with.

What is a source? Living as I now do in Scotland, I look north-east, to author, traveller, hillwalker and educational pioneer Nan Shepherd. In *The Living Mountain*, her celebration of the Cairngorms, Shepherd writes about the Wells of Dee: 'Like all profound mysteries, it is so simple that it frightens me. It wells from the rock, and flows away. For unnumbered years it has welled from the rock, and flowed away. It does nothing, absolutely nothing, but be itself.' The sounds of these syllables are lovely – but what does this piece of writing say? Whatever it means to say, this prose, like poetry, also is a way of saying. Soundscape matters, in nature and in language. Short, repeated phrases suggest, perhaps, the breathing of the climber who rests, awestricken, on the plateau. Perhaps the phrasing suggests how water and its flow are alike but non-identical in their movement from moment to moment, and in their materiality from moment to moment.

The change of tense from 'wells' to 'has welled', followed by the 'It does nothing [...] but be', shows the humility of an ecocritical sensibility, not Romanticism. Human creatures are not the measure of nature's magnitude; not dominant, nor dominated, but alongside, amidst. As W.H. Auden alleges of poetry, in his famous 1939 memorial for W.B. Yeats – that it makes nothing happen – Nan Shepherd's descriptive prose makes absolutely nothing happen; except that in that nothing, the sickness of individualism, with its desire for event and anecdote, falls by the way.

I do not believe that Nan Shepherd's language is patterned simply to convey 'wonder' – not even a great and new wonder informed by mid-twentieth-century mysticism, and 'eastern' ideas of wholeness or interconnexion. Not published until 1977, *The Living Mountain* was written during and just after the Second World War. Perhaps the parameters of Nan Shepherd's imagination are not that dissimilar to Samuel Beckett's in *Endgame*, even if tone and setting could not be more different. Beckett's characters live indoors. Their outdoors is destroyed and inaccessible. Yet Nell, the old woman who dies in her bin, reminisces about a beautiful lake – in her memory lives the source.

I would suggest that the potential of absolute annihilation, whether of human nature or the natural world, which Nan Shepherd's generation came to know through the Shoah and the nuclear bomb, powers the fear with which Shepherd's narrator regards the water. For the human observer is small and properly mortal, in her view of this origin point of a river. The human element could be subtracted from the scene, right then, or forever – neither would matter more or less. Continuity rests with the watery element.

And returning to York, I still hear the delayed fall of raindrops silvering off winter twigs in St Nicks nature reserve, which generously hosts and encourages creative responses to conservation activities. St Nicks hides away near the city centre, but should not be overlooked. The site of a former midden, it has been reclaimed as a marvel of green, toxins tamped down by a layer of clay. An earlier age saw the rivers politely forced into culverts to create a pleasant place for citizens to take their leisure. This exacerbated flood risk. The biodiversity of the banks is being enriched and the flow of water widened and freed, to mitigate flood risk. Becca's workshops collaged contemporary poetry with old newspaper accounts of water behaviour. St Nicks staff ensured that there were some smoothly accessible routes, and spaces to be alone; 'nature writing' never should have been the preserve of the able-bodied, gregarious and wordy... We listened to the soundscape and wrote what we thought we heard onto contoured maps – alinguistic rills of syllables, dialect, the lovely failure of the humanly apprehended translation of the voice of place.

Unlocked

ROD MENGHAM

The city-mound of Roman Poetovio looms over the later Slovenian city of Ptuj. All of its buildings, including the fortified base camp of the Thirteenth Legion, have been levelled. Yet its elevation remains the same as that of Ptuj's medieval castle which survives intact. When I climbed the mound in the early July of 2024, there were fragments of marble bas-reliefs here and there, and the footings of legionary fortifications, all the way to the top – where a fresh excavation was laying bare the pebble foundations of a sanctuary wall. From here there was a long view of the course of the Drava, a river that flows from the Alps into the Danube. Here it is wide and fast-flowing, but not far downstream there is – or was – a strategic crossing point, which is why the Romans dug in right here, establishing a regional capital with a population of 40,000. (Today's inhabitants number only 23,000.)

The medieval and modern city developed alongside the ruins of Poetovio, and hardly encroached on the far bank until the middle of the twentieth century. Yet it is on this western bank that some of the most significant remains have been found, revealing that many of the inhabitants – of all ranks – were adherents to the cult of Mithras. Twenty-two Mithraic shrines have been discovered so far, and there may be others out there. Mithras was the favoured deity of army personnel, and there are good reasons why. Every legionary was contractually bound to twenty years of service. Few survived that long, but Mithras offered redemption to those who kept to their side of the bargain – he was the divine witness, mysteriously present at the signing of every sort of contract.

The Thirteenth Legion was canny with its investments. In the year 69 A.D., when there was an imperial succession crisis, it declared in favour of Vespasian. He was one of their own, having proved himself brutally successful as Legate of the Second Legion during the invasion of Britannia in 43 A.D., and more recently, in quelling the Jewish rebellion of 66 A.D. in Judaea. Only three years later, the Thirteenth Legion was betting on a winner in putting him forward as candidate for Emperor.

But although Mithras was an effective oath-binding agent, offering a bargain afterlife to adherents, he came from the East, bringing with him strong elements of mystery. In the Persian tradition from which he emerged, Mithras was the light behind the mountains, always just beneath the horizon, ever wakeful and ever watchful. No shadow was cast in his realm.

A certain amount of mystery is still attached to the Mithraic shrines. They succeed in repelling all but a very few of their would-be visitors. They succeeded in repelling me, in 2018, when I came to take part in the impressive 'Days of Wine and Poetry' festival, an extraordinary event in which the locals sit happily through hours of esoteric poetry in several languages. Faced with this receptiveness, one might think that the attitudes and expectations of an ancient esoteric religion have somehow percolated and survived through the intervening millennia. Perhaps. In any case, Ptuj is a place where the most important messages are hidden, yielding only to those who persist in seeking the truth, and who enlist the help of an interpreter. I didn't have such help in 2018, when I trudged across the footbridge over the Drava and got lost among the proliferating cul-de-sacs of suburban Ptuj – in search of Mithraeum number III. Only two Mithraea, I and III, have been fully excavated and conserved inside modern buildings constructed in pseudo-classical style. (Some of the finds from Mithraeum V are exhibited – bizarrely – inside the lobby of the aptly-named Hotel Mitra, in the centre of town). I found Mithraeum III in its own little cul-de-sac, locked and bolted, and projecting an aura of sullen neglect. Before I could turn away, there was a roar of several motorbike engines, announcing the approach of four bikers, all kitted out as Hell's-Angel lookalikes. It crossed my mind they were there to renew Mithraic tradition with a ritual sacrifice, but they all piled into the poky little bar at the entrance to the cul-de-sac. Band of brothers, bonding rituals, scars of membership, gang wars – it was as if the place itself was seeding the legionary traditions of mutual allegiance, death and honour (but not obedience to the Emperor – this was the European Union). As I made a tactical retreat back into suburbia, there was a crash of breaking glass and raised voices in the bar. To those about to get hammered, we salute you. From a distance.

Ignominy was my part in that campaign. But I was stubbornly determined to try again. Six years later I returned, enlisting the help of Aleš Šteger – doyen of Slovenian poets, novelist and protagonist of a remarkable series of written-on-site projects. Aleš lives in the capital, Ljubljana, but is a native of Ptuj, and just about everyone there knows him or knows of him. Including Aleksandra Nestorovic, the exceptional Curator of Archaeology at the Regional Museum. Aleksandra is a polymath: and polymathic to a high degree. We arranged to meet at Mithraeum I, the shrine furthest from town, and thence to walk to Mithraeum III, followed by more walking along an obscure footpath and footbridge, back to the centre of town. This in itself was promising: the distance was several miles, allowing plenty of time for peripatetic walking and thinking.

Aleksandra's walking gear consisted of a stylish trouser suit, a billowing silk scarf, a wide-brimmed hat and a wide-brimmed smile. It quickly became clear that she was a living archive of the Mithraic subculture and of its resonances in other traditions of thought. And she excavated the various layers of knowledge that had been shovelled onto the Mithraic sites in order to extricate the genuine article from what was no more than backfill.

Mithraeum I is a large, squarish precinct with several well-preserved courses of stonework and numerous dedication inscriptions. The dedications are all by slaves: well-remunerated slaves whose literacy and numeracy enabled them to operate as customs officials – key personnel in the movement of goods and the extraction of taxes across the empire. In their daily occupation they would have been aware of their place in a large complex system of social strata as well as of religious and ethnic diversity. There is a hefty altarpiece in the sanctuary of Mithraeum I depicting torchbearers who are not wearing Roman headgear, but Phrygian caps. The Mithraic system sees the miscellaneity of human interactions within the wider context of the motions of the planets and the visible stars. The main feature of the altarpiece reproduces the iconic scenario of Mithras sacrificing a bull. Various animals collaborate in this tauricide: a scorpion, a snake, a dog and an eagle, while the known stars look down. Aleksandra pointed out the extraordinary accuracy of the star chart, which includes several stars no longer visible to the naked eye. It was as if the Mithraic point of view was extraterrestrial, seeing the planets from a vantage point outside the solar system. Mithras, who had been born from a rock at the time of the solstice, was destined to keep the balance of the universe.

Aleksandra narrowed down her focus to register the smallest details in the iconographic scheme, and then methodically traced the connections between them all. I felt the aperture of my brain widening to accommodate the expanding field of her research – still obviously underway, still busily in search of the recombinant DNA of this very eclectic religion.

As we walked between Mithraeum I and Mithraeum III, I barely noticed the heat (96 °F) in my enjoyment of the irony – feasibly the greatest living expert on the all-male religion of Mithraism was this female scholar who so clearly relished the challenge. Just to rub it in, Mithraeum III was a macho military sanctuary where the largest altar had been paid for by the armourer Flavius Aper. Once again the image of the bull sacrifice was prevalent. It is worth remembering that the bull would be the largest, most powerful animal you might encounter in the Mediterranean (leaving aside Hannibal's elephants, an aberration). It would also be the most expensive to sacrifice – most celebrants would settle for a hunk of beefsteak, sizzled on the altar. A cut of thigh meat would carry the most prestige.

Aleksandra pointed out the recurrent symbolism of relief carvings in which Mithras is depicted shooting an arrow at a rock in order to release a spring of water. Mithraic shrines are commonly found close to a source of water, she said. I thought immediately of the London Mithraeum, practically on top of the river Walbrook – in the bed of which the earliest writing ever found in the

UK records the freeing of a Roman slave: Tibullus Libertus Venusti (good *praenomen*). Of course – that would have been one contract witnessed by the ever-vigilant Mithras, whose altar was so close by. I guess I had drawn up some sort of contract in 2018 when I promised myself I would come back. I had no idea then of the bureaucratic ritual involved (prior application in writing) and no suspicion it would invoke and animate a female archaeologist to open the portal and let in the light.

We walked to the end of the nearest suburban cul-de-sac and then followed a small path leading in the direction of the Drava. Almost immediately we came across another water source: a spring of fresh water feeding a small pond and stream that coiled around the nearby willows. There were several brown trout lazing in the shallows, a pair of moorhens and – yes: an actual kingfisher, brilliantly blue and gold. We triggered its departure, of course, but not before the scene had settled in our minds as identical to the prospect available to the Romans. It was a far cry from the world of indentures and contracts, but not from the world where you lived every day alongside the animals with a pecking order very similar to theirs – and dreamed every night beneath those enormous skies, with all their slowly turning constellations.

It crossed my mind that Tibullus the poet (d.19 B.C.), whose verses draw on his own extensive military experience, refers in his *Panegyric to Messalla* to the 'tricky Pannonian' (fallax Pannonius), which means he might have been acquainted with this part of the world. Both Tibullus the freed slave and Tibullus the soldier would take a dim view of *fallacitas* – and both knew it was Mithras always listening in when you said one thing but meant another. But Tibullus the poet was technically fallacious when he penned the 'Sulpicia' poems, which ventriloquise a female poetic voice – unless these poems are in fact the work of a female poet. And if this is the case, they are the only poems by a Roman woman we have. The female voice in a male tradition: I have heard one of those unlocking the mysteries of Poetovio.

Auerbach – Artist, Exemplar

DAN BURT

(*i.m.* 1930–2024)

All my paragons have had clay feet, except Frank Auerbach.

He died last week at the age of ninety-three, universally eulogized as 'the greatest living artist'[1] of his time. 'With the death of [Francis] Bacon in 1992 and [Lucian] Freud in 2011, he became a leading contender for the unofficial title "greatest living British artist."'[2] "He will be remembered as an [...] artist whose contribution to portraiture and landscape painting has had no equal during his long lifetime."[3] From this judgment none dissent.

He was not a world-famous artist in 1994 when I was walking down Albemarle Street towards Piccadilly late on an Indian summer's afternoon and a painting of a head in a gallery window arrested me. Frank Auerbach, the name stencilled on Marlborough Gallery's window above the painting, was new to me, a recent émigré to London from D.C. and newcomer to the British art world. With a half hour before the gallery closed, I entered.

On the light grey walls inside hung some twenty paintings, mostly portrait size heads (24" x 24"), a few cityscapes twice that size, and several drawings. All the paintings were heavily impasted, the paint almost sculptural, with thick slashes of black and primary colours scarring the canvases. They were indecipherable until I found the right distance from which to view them; even then heads, figures, streets and buildings were barely discernible. Not all had been sold.

But they rooted in my memory. By 1994 Auerbach had been painting and drawing for some forty-five years. A *succès d'estime* in Britain almost from the first, the London art world – artists, critics, scholars, major collectors – over time increasingly lauded him. Among fellow figurative artists, dubbed the School of London – Michael Andrews, Bacon, Freud, R.B. Kitaj, Leon Kossoff – he was legendary: for his sad childhood, his work habits, above all his artistic practice. He was the only contemporary Lucian Freud collected in depth.

Auerbach's Jewish parents dispatched him, alone, to Britain from Berlin as an eight-year-old refugee in 1938. There for ten years he boarded at Bunce Court, a progressive Quaker school in Kent. The Germans had murdered his parents somewhere in the camps by the end of 1942, leaving Gerda Boehm, a much older cousin in North London, his only living relative.

By the time he graduated from the Royal College of Art in 1955 he had developed the fundamentals of his impast-

---

1 Waldemar Januszczak, *The Sunday Times*, 17 November 2024.
2 *New York Times*, 1 November 2024
3 *The Art Newspaper*, December 2024.

ed, compulsively reworked, almost abstract style of figuration. He had a small circle of sitters, and a few cityscapes, that he drew and painted repeatedly his whole career. Every morning he scraped off or erased what he had painted or drawn the night before, time and again, till the image embodied what he called the 'raw truth'. With paintings this reworking might build up a thick base you could carve with a palette knife; with drawings it often wore holes in the paper he then patched. Both methods created palimpsests one sensed beneath the final image. Such was his style from his debut show at London's Beaux Arts Gallery in 1956 until his death sixty-eight years later.

More than his craft was sui generis. He painted 364 days a year, taking off only Christmas Day. For thirty-three years he lived seven days a week in his one room studio in Camden's Mornington Crescent area; from 1987 until his death he lived there three. Until his last decade he almost invariably refused interviews. Openings, his own included, he gave a miss, likewise dinner parties. He refused a knighthood; after his fame escaped gravity he declined to become a Companion of Honour, explaining that it would have been a distraction, bringing with it unwanted personal attention.

I knew none of this, nor had I met him, when I bought his *Head of Gerda Boehm* (1978–9) at auction in 1996. Sotheby's put it in a 'Day Sale' at which they offer less expensive art than in their evening sales. His paintings which had haunted me since I first saw them at Marlborough came clearly to mind when I saw the *Gerda Boehm* image in Sotheby's catalogue. But the *Gerda Boehm* was even more striking than the paintings I remembered, its guide price a third less. I readied my paddle.

Ever since, the *Head of Gerda Boehm* has hung four feet to the right of my desk. For near three decades I've looked at it every day when I sit down to work. When my eyes lift from my laptop I often swivel to *Gerda Boehm*; never does she age or stale, the hallmark of great art.

During my first decade in London, lawyering and a long-standing interest in art conjoined to involve me deeply in the British art world. I met Kitaj, Paula Rego and Anish Kapoor amongst other noted British artists. But it was to Auerbach I returned most often.

I grew familiar with his oeuvre from seeing it in exhibitions and catalogues. The essays in them, as well as reviews, monographs and occasional interviews taught me about his style, habits and aesthetic aims. From his sitters, dealers, curators, scholars I learned of the physical labour that making his art required, his erudition and his love of poetry. And from all these sources, especially interviews in his last decade, shone his extraordinary articulateness, thoughtfulness and profound understanding of his craft.

Frank Auerbach was no curmudgeonly recluse, no anchorite. Obsession had no purchase on his character. Warm, friendly, a wonderful dinner companion, dedicated. He chose not to travel or socialize because, as he said in one late interview, when he got up in the morning he could think of nothing better to do than paint, and so he did.

Fame did not change him. He had no 'side', never denigrating other artists, sympathetic to poor sinners who must paint for their dinners, to those whose careers never caught fire. He visited museums and galleries at times when there were few other visitors or none, the better to study the art displayed. An artist I knew ran into him more than once at these shows, as did I at the Royal Academy's Hockney Exhibition in May 2017.

Frank and Julia Auerbach at David Hockney Exhibit, 25 May 2017. Photograph by Yvonne Burt

Auerbach often said his goal with each work was to create a living presence, a thing with life independent of its creator. After nearly a decade sitting beside the *Head of Gerda Boehm*, she became for me that living presence. I knew the role Gerda Boehm had played in Auerbach's life after he came to London, learned she'd been one of his regular sitters in the seventies, discovered my *Gerda Boehm* had been one of his paintings that represented Britain in the 1986 Venice Biennale at which he won the *Lion d'Or*. Slowly I began to think I understood the *Head of Gerda Boehm*, and to test that perception I wrote 'Modern Painters'.

> He trowels white, ochre, builds a base,
> carves, smears, slashes, waits...
> with black strokes carves a flayed face
> on the impasted canvas. Next day erase,
> daub on paint again, again efface,
> repeat till a palimpsestic skin's in place
> and the sitter's flesh replaced
> with grey slabs like rotting salmon filets.
>
> We look like this after things fall apart,
> the painting merely an autopsy report
> on the corpse war dumped on the coroner's cart.
> He lifts a palette-knife to start:
> invade, split rib cage, spread thought apart,
> slit pericardium, sound cankered heart,
> anatomize the entrail's parts,
> that heap of faiths and old philosophies
> encasing the mean midden of descent
> and express the ravaged guts of a continent –
> gas chambers, burn pits, barbed wire ligaments –
> slaughter so savage horror itself is spent.
>
> Freighted with these painted lineaments
> the curtain falls on the Enlightenment
> like Luftmenschen[4] ash on the Red regiments
> storming west through Poland from Stalingrad.

---

4 Death camp inmates referred to the ash blowing from the crematoria smokestacks as *Luftmensch(en)* (literally air persons). It is Yiddish for an unworldly, impractical man.

Detail of *Head of Gerda Boehm*. Frank Auerbach. Photograph: Paul Hodgson. Copyright © Estate of Frank Auerbach. Courtesy of Frankie Rossi Gallery

Auerbach was more than the subject of *Modern Painters*, he was an exemplar when I began trying seriously to write poetry. With his oeuvre in mind, I chose the first half of the poem's second stanza's opening line – *We look like this* – as the title of my first poetry collection, and with Auerbach's permission used the *Gerda Boehm* image on its dust jacket.

Courtesy demanded I send him a copy of the book on publication. Therefore despite terror at being revealed as an imposter, I sent him a copy of *We Look Like This*, the *Head of Gerda Boehm* covering the dust jacket, *Modern Painters* inside testifying to my small understanding of his art. A few days later I received the following letter:

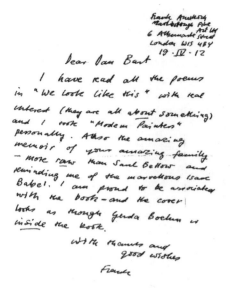

Copyright © Estate of Frank Auerbach

In the last dozen years of Frank Auerbach's life, the ones after I received his note and I came to know him better, he continued to paint and live as he had all his creative life. He developed a late style – less impasted, brighter, easier to read, vibrant – that produced nonpareil work. Skulls began appearing in cityscapes and studio pictures, as age inevitably ambushed him. The plaudits he never chased rained on him. His major retrospective at Tate Britain was rapturously reviewed.

Covid lockdown deprived him of his sitters, so he drew and painted self-portraits and views of his studio which drew clamorous praise. A two-room exhibition last year of his charcoal heads from 1954–6 notched the Courtauld's highest visitor numbers ever for a three-month show.

But painting inexorably became harder as his heart weakened. Two months ago he entered hospital to explore what help surgery might be. "Little" said the doctors. Soon after leaving hospital time pried the brush from his hand. Two weeks later he was dead.

More Truly and More Strange: *Harmonium* at 102

HARRY SANDERSON

When Wallace Stevens published *Harmonium* in 1923 it was strange for a few reasons. He was a relatively unknown New England insurance lawyer, he was releasing his first collection at the age of forty-four, and he was not easily associated with any school or movement. But above all the poems were simply very peculiar, mingling romantic and modernist tendencies in a manner that remains obscure at its centenary. Those who think the older Wallace Stevens spent too long writing in his own manner overlook the fact that he arrived late, not dressed in the appropriate fashion, with the feeling of someone who had been speaking to himself for years.

He also came reluctantly. In 1922 he wrote to *Poetry* magazine editor Harriet Monroe: 'Gathering together the things for my book has been so depressing that I wonder at Poetry's friendliness. All my earlier things seem like horrid cocoons from which later abortive insects have sprung. The book will amount to nothing, except that it may teach me something.' He would later record the 'horror' that attended his reading of proofs. This is distinct from modesty, or the poet's inevitable sense of inadequacy. The hesitance springs from the task Stevens had set himself, addressing a subject that could rarely be conveyed clearly.

That objective is something that can only be hedged at, often in terms Stevens himself employed: imagination, poetry, clarity. His syntax often suggests a philosophical argument, but the constituent disquisitions rarely amount to a plain statement. Take the closing lines of 'Le Monocle de Mon Oncle'

> Every day, I found
> Man proved a gobbet in my mincing world.
> Like a rose rabbi, later, I pursued,
> And still pursue, the origin and course
> Of love, but until now I never knew
> That fluttering things have so distinct a shade.

Even allowing for the camp stylings, there is a vagueness within the sense being driven towards. Helen Vendler called these Stevens's 'qualified assertions', Marjorie Perloff his 'ironic modes'. Stevens is reluctant to provide a sentence that does not demand one accept his own peculiar procedure of thought. That demand cannot be realised, since it was the incomprehensibility of the imagined world that preoccupied him:

> My titillations have no footnotes
> And their memorials are the phrases
> Of idiosyncratic music

The lack of referents refuses neat resolution just as music resists prose paraphrase: the poems forever announce clarity of meaning, but linger in the twilight of suggestion. This side of *Harmonium* can feel like a labyrinth when subject to second-hand analysis. But when read, it is a collection thick in melodies, perfumes and libidinal excess:

> Gloomy grammarians in golden gowns,
> Meekly you keep the mortal rendezvous,
> Eliciting the still sustaining pomps
> Of speech which are like music so profound
> They seem an exaltation without sound.
> Funest philosophers and ponderers,
> Their evocations are the speech of clouds.

This is the dandy at the harmonium, dramatic persona to the kitschiness of high modernism and rococo.

Nature folds into language, then back again, in exotic scales of diction: Peter Quince is at the clavier, the Prince of Peacocks meets Berserk, the Emperor of Ice Cream rolls big cigars, villagers dream of baboons and periwinkles. There is a Hymn from the Watermelon Pavilion, three girls plot against a giant, the third resolving to 'whisper / Heavenly labials in a world of gutturals'. *Harmonium* is something between a gnostic gospel, a field guide to the unconscious, and a book of spells.

I am convinced that there is an argument we can ultimately construe given enough concentration and spiritual development, possibly with the aid of technology. I have no way of proving this, of course, and may have been bamboozled by a fraud – but there are times when one is content to be caught in a trap, and reading *Harmonium* is one of them.

Where is it at 100? Still bearing unresolved riddles for academics: the *Wallace Stevens Journal*'s centenary edition is full of forensic insight. Influential on the last century of poetry, particularly in America: Harry Mathews hears the 'heartfelt noise of harmoniums at dusk', and Stevens echoes through John Ashbery's early romantic work. Younger American poets Timothy Donnelly and Rowan Ricardo Phillips, each of whom published collections this year, speak in a language that Stevens devised.

But there is, too, a risk that *Harmonium* set a pace of philosophical interrogation which its disciples could not sustain. The obscurity of *Harmonium* may have given a licence for obscurantism, so that long-read *Reviews of Books* now come covered in the free verse of Stevens scholars which contain all of the theorising, but none of the fun.

Harmonium serves as an antidote to many of the ills of contemporary poetry, which can tend towards the digestible at the expense of the queer, the confessional at the expense of the authentic, resistant to the indivisibility of the subject and its imagined world. In an early review, the poet Shaemas O'Scheel said of some *Harmonium* pieces that they were 'untruthful, and nauseating to read'. Poets that lay claim to truth are generally boring, and nauseating lyrics are, within reason, something to be looked into. At times it seems that Stevens is either forgotten or forsaken. We hope that he simply remains late, always promising to arrive soon.

The Warwick Prize for Nelly Sachs

ANDREW SHANKS

Andrew Shanks has won the 2024 Warwick Prize for Women in Translation with *Revelation Freshly Erupting* by Nelly Sachs.

The £1,000 prize was established by the University of Warwick in 2017 to address the gender imbalance in translated literature and to increase the number of international women's voices accessible to British and Irish readers. The prize was judged by Amanda Hopkinson, Boyd Tonkin and Susan Bassnett.

In accepting the prize, Andrew Shanks (his brief talk, laid out in the form he uses to phrase out sermons, should not be confused with an attempt at verse!) said:

Nelly Sachs was a German Jew.
As late as the middle of May 1940,
    she, and her mother, were still in Berlin,
        anxiously awaiting the Swedish entry visa
            that they needed.
The day they escaped, by plane, to Stockholm,
    Nazi tanks were racing through France,
        breaking through the border defences of Belgium,
        circulating freely through the Netherlands.
She was forty-eight.
She'd previously just dabbled in literature.
It was the trauma of exile which made her a great poet.

I've been translating Sachs's work
    for over forty years now, on and off.
I first came across it one idle afternoon,
    whilst browsing in a bookshop
        in Marburg an der Lahn,
            where I was living at the time.
I'd never heard of her.
In my experience, not many
    English-speaking people have.
And yet, in 1966 she was awarded
    the Nobel Prize for Literature.

For a long time, I was translating her
    just for my own pleasure.
It was Michael Schmidt of Carcanet Press
    who suggested that, if they were tidied up a bit,
        my versions
            might well be publishable.
I'm most grateful to him.
There are older translations, done in the later 1960s.
But my approach is much freer.
And I'm hoping that what I've produced
    might be a bit more successful
        in drawing attention to her...

It's perhaps misleading to call Sachs a 'religious poet'.
She's certainly not a conventional one,
    in terms of any particular doctrinal tradition.
But I'm, by trade, a philosophical theologian.
And, to me, she seems to be
    one of the *religiously* most interesting poets
        of modern times...

And now I'll read you my translation
    of the short poem
        which she herself chose to read
            at the Nobel Prize award ceremony.

It dates from 1957, and is an example of her later style.
She calls her later poems 'riddles':
    they're ultra-compacted bodies of metaphor.
This 'riddle' belongs to a collection
    entitled 'Flight and Metamorphosis'
'Flight' in the double sense of fleeing, and soaring.
'Metamorphosis' of the soul.
It's a sacramental poem.
It speaks of itself, as a 'stone' holding a fossil-insect in it.
In the bourgeois world of her childhood and youth,
    collecting such stones was a very fashionable pastime.
There's an allusion to a fish: always, for her,
    a figure of mute affliction.
Also, an 'ailing butterfly' – the poet herself.
And the sea: at once, I think,
    both death and eternal life...

It goes like this:

> For the fugitive
> what wealth of welcome
> on the way –
> Enveloped
> in the cloth of winds
> feet fixed within the prayer of sand
> which never reaches its amen
> for it must pass
> by way of fin to wing
> and then beyond –
>
> The ailing butterfly's
> no stranger to the sea –
> This stone
> inscribed with insect-speech
> was placed into my hand –
>
> Deprived of home
> I hold the transformations of the world –

Set 8: Mondo de Katastrofoj

TRANSLATED BY JOHN GALLAS

1.
Life like tooth
             Boris Vian (1920–1959/France)

life like tooth
not much bother to start with
bing I'm hungry bong I'm thirsty
suddenly ow bursty-bursty
pain like you never thought nothing else matters
worry worry call the doctor please
can't be helped incurable disease
pull it out extract extract extract the end

2.
like always like forever
             Anonymous (early 20th Century/Paiute song)

like always   like forever
snow holds   the hills
the deer   the high-horn
stalk down   tracking
the south sun   wattlebeans
and clumpgrass
                    thunderdrums
blast in   the hill tents
like always   like forever
we snap   sage seeds
dry deermeat   summerskinned
sick of   our squats
our smokestenched   shirts
sick for   the south sun
and limber   hillgrass

3.
A Brazilian Tragedy
             Manuel Bandeira (1886–1968/Brazil)

Misael, 63, Civil Servant, Ministry of Labour, met Maria Elvira, prostitute, syphilis, ulcerated fingers, pawned wedding-ring, poor-girl's teeth.

Misael removed Maria from her *vale of tears,* put her in a two-storey house in Estácio, paid for the doctor, the dentist and the manicurist... anything she wanted, he got her.

When Maria Elvira saw herself with lovely new teeth, she went out to get a lover.

Misael kept things quiet. He could have hit her, shot, knifed her. But he didn't. They just moved. So it went for three years: Maria Elvira found a new lover, they moved.

Misael and Elvira lived in Estácio, Rocha, Catete, General Pedra Street, Olaria, Ramos, Bonsucesso, Vila Isabel, Marquês de Sapucaí Street, Niterói, Encantado, Clapp Street, again in Estácio, Todos os Santos, Catumbi, Lavradio, Boca do Mato, Inválidos...

They ended up in Constituição Street, where Misael, probably losing his temper, shot her six times. She was found by the Police dead on her back, in a blue organdy dress.

4.
A Poem from Noto
          Anonymous (Eighth Century/
      Japan)

O O he's dropped his axe, his precious axe,
in the river where it's all muddy
and the Kumaki waves slosh you off your feet.
O O he's dropped his axe.

O O he's doing his nut, he's losing it:
O mud melt softly, O waves stop sloshing,
and when all's quiet we'll see,
we'll see if it floats to the top.

5.
Our car drove ...
        Hans Davidsohn (1887–1942/Jewish-German)

Our car drove into the Goldfish Pond.
The water came up to our knees.
We said goodbye and got ready to die.
The sun looked on through the trees.

O I shall be true in the cold, wet grave!
I cried. (We had started to sink).
But the Fire Truck came and pulled us out,
And the sky went yellow and pink.

       *

6.
The Girl with the Golden Voice
      Jean Lorrain (1855–1906/France)

So the fife *squeals* and *Zim-Boom* the cymbal
smacks, and *hey presto!* amidst the belches,
screams, howls, in the foul halo of the oil-lamps,
the goddess appears.
                        Her triumphal train
blanch-white satin, her skin so gorgeous and frail
amidst gigantic bunches of flowers,
gaspingly pale, slap-whore style,
that she looks like a starveling beam of moonlight.
                                    Starwise
the goddess comes forth, frosted and glittery:
she sings – suddenly her voice rasps and shrieks
like a shot accordion, and *ooh-ooh!* above the crowd
white confetti softly falls: the voice cracks, broken glass –
the crowd giggles and hoots – and off they go,
leaving... leaving the Ice Queen... crowned with snow.

Letter from Wales

SAM ADAMS

I did not make a note of it at the time and now can no longer recall when I bought Joseph Wright's *English Dialect Dictionary*, or indeed what prompted me to do so. All I can vouch for is that it was many years ago and not a random act. I have used it from time to time – as one does dictionaries – but mostly the six hefty volumes occupy their fourteen inches of shelf space, a calm steady presence. Together they weigh just short of three stones. The dictionary claims to be 'the complete vocabulary of all dialect words still in use, or known to have been in use during the last two hundred years' – a bold boast where living language is concerned. It was published in 1905, in London, by Henry Frowde, Amen Corner, E.C., and in New York by Putnam's Sons, having already been issued in parts at intervals from June 1898. An enormous undertaking, it involved hundreds of contributing correspondents, mostly from England, but including fifteen from Ireland, six from Scotland and five from Wales, three of whom came from English-speaking south Pembrokeshire. The bibliography contains nine references to Wales, one of which refers the reader to 'Shropshire', compared with twelve double-column pages for Scotland. No doubt the problem for Wright was that Wales, especially the rural north and west, was still at that time predominantly Welsh-speaking, and of the few correspondents he recruited here, judging from their surnames, most were English incomers. Similarly, a chapter on pronunciation recognises 'a sound like *ch* in German *ich*, *nach*, *noch*... common in Shetland, Orkney and Scotland in words like "bright"...', but does not identify a similar, stronger *ch* in Welsh. When, during the early years of the Second World War, teachers were evacuated from Chatham in Kent to Gilfach Goch, they confounded locals by referring to the village as 'Gilffa Go'. But of course Wright was referring to English words. Among the preliminary pages is a list of counties from which dialect words were harvested that includes all thirteen original (pre-1975) counties of Wales, except Monmouthshire and Glamorgan. Perhaps Wright erroneously considered Monmouthshire English, or 'south Wales' was meant to embrace those two, while 'north Wales' served the counties of Y Gogledd, which are, however, separately listed. It's a fiddling matter, especially since identifying a Welsh coinage or usage in the dictionary is not much easier than finding needles in haystacks. And then there is the curious case of 'Cy'. According to the list of abbreviations, 'n.Cy.' means 'north Country'. Could it have been the original intention to employ 'Cy.' for Cymru (Wales), but in this landslide of words the notion became confused and lost?

Other items have left me pondering – and doubtful. For example, 'accabe' is listed as a south Pembrokeshire word expressing disgust, probably of Lower German origin, 'being due to the Flemish colonists in Pembroke [...] The Holstein Idiotikon [...] has 'akkefi!' [...] an expression [...] employed by nurses to dirty little children.' What Wright's correspondent heard, and his own etymological studies perhaps mistakenly informed, is still used everywhere in Wales, 'Ach y fi', and with the same meaning. I find it hard to accept that so common an expression was imported and that it spread so widely. Perhaps the Flemish colonists absorbed and adopted it from the Welsh. The word 'bap', for a small soft roll of bread, has its origins in Scotland and Ireland. 'Boggy-bo', for 'a ghost, a hobgoblin' comes from Yorkshire and Cheshire, but 'Bugan' for 'an evil spirit' is clearly from the Welsh *bwgan*, which means much the same. I assumed 'butty' for a friend or workmate was Welsh, for I have never heard or seen it in any English context, yet Wright says it is in general dialect use in England. 'Cantred', the word for 'a measure of land', is said to be from Ireland, but 'cantref', the ancient Welsh word with identical meaning, does not appear.

A word like 'tally' arrived here with incomers, like my grandfather, from over the border. It was an early equivalent of paying for goods by instalments and came to be applied in the phrase 'living tally' to designate a couple living together unmarried. I cannot forbear adding, courtesy of Wright, that to folk in south Cheshire and north-west Derbyshire, 'tally-wag' meant 'membrum virile'. Then there is the problem with 'Taffy' – now a common, even friendly term for a Welshman, which I assumed was somehow derived from 'David' ('Dafydd' in Welsh). But the dictionary tells us that from Cumbria to Wiltshire a 'Taffy' is a 'weak-minded, thoughtless, irresolute person; a simpleton'. That, presumably, is the result of the English never having learned to speak Welsh. There are many other unexpected meanings. 'Whelk' for instance had nothing to do with shellfish, but in Cornwall and Derbyshire it was 'a sty on the eyelid', which could be cured 'by passing a black cat's tail nine times over the place'. In parts of northern England and Scotland, a 'wooster' was 'a lover', and a 'wooster blister' a slap on the face. What would Hollywood make of 'Werwolf', which to Wright's informants meant 'a puny child; an undergrown person of any age'?

I have been scurrying through the biography of Wright by his wife, Elizabeth (Lea), now available online. It reveals the great love and respect they had for one another and also the extent to which the dictionary was a shared endeavour. Joseph Wright was born in 1855. His birthplace, Idle, now absorbed into the suburbs of Bradford, Yorkshire, was then a sizeable village. His father was a cloth weaver and quarry worker, his mother took in washing and 'charred', and, as a six-year-old, Joseph was set to work leading a donkey cart carrying tools at the quarry. His only schooling was as a 'half-timer' and he left that before his thirteenth birthday knowing only the alphabet, some Bible passages and moral verses by heart, and basic arithmetic. Hearing newspaper accounts of the 1870 Franco-Prussian War read aloud by a workmate at the woollen mill prompted him to teach himself to read. Once started he devoted himself to learning: night school three nights a week for sixpence, Cassell's *Popular Educator* at seven pence a part. In 1876, with money saved, he enrolled at the University of Heidelberg, walking there from Antwerp. His education continued at the Yorkshire College of Science (later Leeds University) and Heidelberg again, where in 1885 he gained a doctorate. In 1888 he became a lecturer at the Taylorian in Oxford, and in 1901 he was appointed Professor of Comparative Philology at Oxford University.

Features

from Appa Stories

SUJATA BHATT

Mosquitoes

Appa has warned the children about mosquitoes, but they are not impressed. They're afraid of bats and snakes, not mosquitoes. After Appa has finished speaking, the children ask him to say 'mosquito' again.

The children enjoy asking Appa to say 'mosquito'; he pronounces it 'moss-quito', which makes them laugh. Already the children have a different accent when they speak English. But no matter how much English they learn, they will always call their father 'Appa'.

Bats and Snakes

Now, Appa stands in the veranda, the indigo sky behind him, he is about to enter the house. The children are restless beside him; he urges them to go indoors, away from the mosquitoes.

Appa doesn't know that the children have just escaped from the bats, or so they feel. The children have a special zigzag way of running, which, they believe, not only protects them from bats, but also from snakes. Once again, this evening, the children feel that the bats would have flown into their ears, and then would have remained stuck forever within their heads if they hadn't managed to escape in time. How and why the children have come to believe that bats want to fly into their ears is a mystery that even the children cannot fully explain. If Appa were to question them regarding this matter, they would say that they just know these things about bats.

For one thing, Appa tells the children that he cannot understand how such large bats could squeeze themselves into their ears. And why would they even want to? After all, bats prefer caves. Now what about snakes, Appa wonders, have the children ever seen snakes? No. The children shake their heads, they've never seen any snakes. But that doesn't prevent them from believing that there are millions of snakes living in their garden. Millions and millions, the children say, but we know how to trick them and even if they follow us, we can run faster.

'You know, Appa,' the youngest adds, 'the snakes really do follow us. I know that they are giant snakes because I can hear them, and they sound like giant snakes.'

And then he shows Appa his special style of running.

The Other Country

The children have arrived in Poona with a New Orleans accent and a modern, relatively advanced vocabulary that is alien to their classmates. Their syntax is different too. It will always remain so. Their teachers are appalled by this accent and suspicious of their vocabulary. Where did they learn to speak like that?

The other country, where the children have been living, has become one of their own and will always remain so. The children find it natural to have multiple countries.

White Blood Cells

When the children fall and run home with bleeding elbows and knees, Appa says, 'don't cry. Now, now, stop crying. Your white blood cells will help you. Your white blood cells will start working now. Stop crying. Now go and wash it out with soap.' And that really makes the children quiet. Stunned. They try to imagine their white blood cells as they peer at their bright red knees.

The eldest remembers Appa's anatomy book. How the blood flows one way and then another. Red, blue, red: so, the arteries and veins are coloured. Appa has explained the function of the heart and the lungs to the children and has told them how the blood must flow unhampered. Always.

Flies

The eldest remembers a time when she thought flies were harmless, friendly creatures. That was when she was four and the youngest was still a baby. She remembers watching a fly sitting beside a sliced tomato in the kitchen, how a few green seeds were floating in the watery juice. She remembers watching the fly rub its fine, filament hands, and then, how it rubbed its face. She watched and watched, and even started to speak with the fly until Appa rushed up to her and scolded her for playing with a fly. 'Flies are dangerous', he informed her. 'Flies are full of diseases, and they will make you very sick', he warned. Never again did the eldest look kindly upon a fly.

How Appa Deals with Flies

No one can beat Appa at killing flies. Four, five, six flies dead within seconds. No chance for them to escape Appa's powerful swipes with the fly swatter. Appa is always fast in everything that he does. Nonetheless, the children rarely see him move as quickly as he does when he's killing flies.

Appa could be a brilliant tennis player if he wanted to. The children enjoy watching him as he sprints across the room. They're impressed with the way he leaps and twirls – suddenly jumping high, then swooping down low when no one expects it. Often Appa smashes a fly dead in mid-air then catches it on the fly swatter before it falls to the floor. Back and forth he goes and then around the table where the children are sitting quietly waiting for their dinner.

The fly swatter is a whizzing blur surrounding them. The children are too tired to help Appa. Besides he has told them not to move – and furthermore, as the eldest says, Appa is the best at killing flies. She is certain that the flies are terrified of Appa and his strength, and of course his fierce determination. The eldest is convinced that sometimes one stern look from Appa is enough to disorient the flies and send them into a bewildered state of weakness and paralysis – which makes it even easier for him to kill them.

The flies have no enemy greater than Appa. The eldest says that flies are not sufficiently afraid of children. The youngest nods in agreement.

Washing Hands

Appa always washes his hands very carefully after killing flies, although he avoids touching them. In fact, Appa washes his hands more frequently than anyone else in the world. The children begin to wash their hands frequently as well, especially the eldest.

The Children Would Like to Be Friends with the Monkeys

Actually, the children would like to be friends with the monkeys, but the monkeys have different ideas. The problem is that the monkeys do not really care for the children. The monkeys like to tease the children, and the children like to tease the monkeys. It's an endless game. The children think the monkeys throw gulmohar leaves and flowers to them out of kindness, but the monkeys don't see it that way.

Rabies

Appa has told the children about rabies. He has told them to stay away from monkeys. He has warned them many times. But no one has told the monkeys to stay away from the children. If Appa knew that sometimes the children eat gulmohar leaves thrown down to them by monkeys in the trees, then he might even faint, the children believe, and afterwards he would give them more injections.

Dr. Work's Leopard

The children are delighted because they have also been invited along with Appa and Ma to a dinner party at Dr. Work's house. Their friend Amrit, Dr. Work's daughter who is around the same age as the eldest, will also be there. The children remember visiting the Works at their home when they were all in their other country. They had such a wonderful time together. Amrit and the eldest spent a lot of time searching for fairy dust and Peter Pan. The youngest helped too.

All the children have a fervent wish to be able to fly which unfortunately has never been fulfilled. 'We just have to keep searching for fairy dust', the eldest says. Amrit and the youngest agree although it is very tiring work to sift through rocks and sand, sticks and leaves while searching for fairy dust. On top of that they have been running uphill and down for quite a while now. The eldest wants to know where Peter Pan really, really lives. Amrit and the youngest say it's a secret. No one knows.

Dr. Work from California has returned to Poona; he keeps a leopard in his house. These are the days when 'Pune' is still 'Poona' and still very, very green. The leopard is tame but nonetheless wild. Mrs. Work rescued it after hunters killed its mother; the leopard was a baby then, but now it's grown up.

Dr. Work's house is very large, and the garden seems spacious enough for a leopard. But the eldest thinks that the leopard might prefer its very own private jungle. The children have never been so close to a leopard before. It's scary and exciting they think as they look at each other and at the leopard.

It is a wonderful dinner party. There are a few other children with their parents. The children wonder whether the leopard likes dinner parties or any other sort of parties. Mrs. Work says that the leopard has already eaten. The eldest wonders how often the leopard likes to eat.

The children don't believe the leopard is tame.

'I tell you it has a leopard's heart and a leopard's mind. It knows that it's still a real leopard and it wants to be real leopard. It will never be tame', the eldest tells the other children.

The younger ones are quiet. Amrit smiles. They're supposed to finish their dinner, but they can't. They simply stare at the leopard pacing in front of them. The children stare at the leopard, but the leopard doesn't stare back at the children. It's probably good that he's not so interested in us, the eldest thinks.

Everyone's parents are eating in another room, a room without a leopard.

Appa is talking about viruses with Dr. Work again. The mothers don't want to hear about diseases while they're eating. They want to talk about flowers; let's discuss something pleasant, they say. The eldest can hear everything. The rooms are open and spacious. But the leopard doesn't explore the other rooms. Maybe he's afraid that Dr. Work will scold him, the eldest thinks to herself. Although Dr. Work is a very fun-loving, kind man, still the eldest reasons he probably has to be firm with the leopard.

Appa and Dr. Work have worked together for quite a few years, long before the children were born. They are passionate about viruses – and hunting them down, the children know. That's what they call research.

Many years will pass before the children realize what pioneers they were: Dr. Work and Appa. 'What amazing discoveries they made! Ground-breaking is an understatement!', the children will tell each other when they are grown up and reading about Appa's projects with Dr. Work. 'They really did the impossible! Or what was considered impossible in those days.' But Appa and Dr. Work will no longer be around to comment.

The leopard paces in its own area which is quite large, and it has a huge window to look out of. The leopard stays close to the window. Continuously pacing. The leopard never tires.

'It needs lots of space', the eldest says. The youngest agrees. 'Maybe it wants to go hunting. Look it's already dark outside. Leopards like to stay awake all night. They're not like dogs, you know.'

Actually, the children would like to be friends with the leopard, but they don't know how they could ever manage to do that. How can one manage to be friends with such a wild animal – even if it lives with the Work family? The children have to admit to themselves that ultimately even the monkeys don't want to be friends with them, so how can they gain the trust of a leopard? How can they understand the feelings of a leopard? For one thing they are afraid of the leopard.

Appa, on the other hand, is not afraid of the leopard; he's not worried that the children are eating dinner with a leopard. Dr. Work's leopard is certainly clean, free of viruses and bacteria.

A Silvery Metal Star

Swallowing a metal star results in the eldest having to eat eight bananas all at once. That is Appa's solution when he is informed at his office. The eldest doesn't know how she manages to eat eight bananas all at once. It must be fear, fear that drives her on to fulfil Appa's orders; she knows that Appa must be terribly annoyed with her for doing such a silly thing. How their mother obtains eight bananas is another mystery. Perhaps, Mrs. Rao, who has ample supplies of everything, simply gave them to her. An emergency is an emergency, and there's no time to waste.

Dr. Rao and the Cockroaches

Appa tells the children that Dr. Rao is an entomologist.
'Oh! What is that?!' the children ask.
'An entomologist is someone who studies insects', Appa explains.
'Oh!' the eldest says again, 'Oh!'

Actually, she's not sure what to say. To herself she thinks, 'now why would anyone want to do that? Study insects?!' But she doesn't say that. She knows that Appa always has clever explanations for everything. The youngest finds it hilarious to imagine Dr. Rao studying insects.

'Well, I do like butterflies and dragonflies', the eldest says, trying not to dismiss all insects. 'Bees are important but they're too dangerous', the eldest adds.

'Worms are funny', the youngest says.

'I don't know,' the eldest replies, 'maybe some of them are funny like the green inchworms in New Orleans. Remember the green inchworms?' They all remember the green inchworms.

'Dr. Rao is very skilful,' Appa continues, 'he knows how to give injections to cockroaches.' Now the children find Dr. Rao's activities truly bizarre. They make faces showing their shock and disgust. The only injections the children receive are vaccinations, they don't know of any other type of injections, so, naturally they think the cockroaches are receiving vaccinations too. The children imagine hundreds of cockroaches in Dr. Rao's office crawling all over the floor and on to his desk as they wait patiently to receive an injection from him. The children simply cannot understand why such a nice, friendly man like Dr. Rao who loves parties and ice-cream just as much as they do would want to spend so much time in close proximity to cockroaches. The children suppose that Appa is unable to give injections to cockroaches.

'Just as well,' the eldest thinks, 'what a horrible chore that must be.'

The children are happy and relieved that Appa doesn't spend time with cockroaches.

'At least Appa is always looking for viruses,' the eldest says to the youngest, 'that's more exciting because viruses are invisible.' The youngest agrees.

The children know that vaccinations are meant to help people, and that ultimately no matter how unpleasant it is to receive an injection, vaccinations prevent one from getting the disease. Appa has explained this to them on several occasions.

The children think Dr. Rao is a very kind man for wanting to help cockroaches with their cockroach diseases. Well, they always knew he was very kind, but it seems to them that his kindness has no limits since it even extends to cockroaches.

They wonder if the cockroaches seek him out or if he goes looking for cockroaches that need help. Maybe he has to persuade them to get injections.

They imagine that Mrs. Rao like most people would not want the cockroaches or any other insects to visit Dr. Rao in their home.

'Mrs. Rao is very normal', the eldest says.

The youngest nods and says, 'Maybe she doesn't know that Dr. Rao spends so much time with cockroaches'.

'Now why would cockroaches need vaccinations? Do they really have so many cockroach diseases?' The eldest wonders and looks at the youngest who merely shrugs, equally mystified.

The children are relieved that Ma keeps their house so clean that no cockroaches, let alone any other insect, would dare to enter. Of course, there are flies sometimes but Appa knows how to get rid of them.

Mrs. Rao also keeps the Rao family home immaculate, so the children wonder where Dr. Rao finds his cockroaches.

'Maybe somewhere out in the jungle', the youngest says. The eldest agrees. The jungle is far away but it does exist.

The children are too shy and embarrassed to ask Dr. Rao about the cockroaches. They instinctively sense that there must be something more to it than what Appa has told them and rightly believe it would be too complicated for them to understand.

Three Poems

TARA BERGIN

The Process

Everything starts in the field – some thistles, say, or a bunch of moss.
These get reformed into bandages. Then spitting cloths.
Then the ragman turns the spitting cloths into paper.

Enter me, the 'maker'.

I purchase paper from the ragman by the hundred sheet pack.
I fill every sheet front and back, then I place the sheets in stacks
for the Nightmen.

When the Nightmen come they buy my jottings for a decent sum.
They don't read them. No need.
They twist the paper into wrappings for tobacco, weed –

worse stuff – roofies, golden girls, bad bean.

When the Nightmen get arrested, as they often do,
no one ever questions you-know-who –
even when I tell them to.

Even when I stand in the station and ring the bell.

I say: I'm sure my words are culpable!

But the officers reply from their neon lair:
Madam, you need to get this clear.
Whatever you've written? Makes no difference here.

Charlotte in Aesthetics

Charlotte in aesthetics says
that to remove a tattoo
she has to laser the skin.
The laser picks up the ink
and thinks it's hair –
then it burns the ink off at the root.

Charlotte says it plain like that because
clients need to know
there will be pain and bleeding.

Charlotte says that everyone cries
at some stage during proceedings.

Even the men with tribal signs around their waist.
Even the men with cunt on their arm.
Even the men with tears.

Grief / Installation Piece

For years we thought this kind of thing was imperious and very distant.
Then we found it was contemporary – very much of our time.

Looking at it more carefully
we saw that it had of course all the characteristics of modernity:

seriality; mundanity; the shock effect;
the way the common object is taken out of context.

It caused terrible conflict, both among us as a group
and within each of us individually.

We wondered whether this was the intention.

My own impression was of a grey field with twelve grey tombs.
It was steely, and somewhat cold.

I didn't love it.
I didn't want it.
I didn't even like looking at it.

But I can't deny the impact it had on me.

I mean some days

I think I might never get over it.

At Swim-Three-Tongues

ANDREW McNEILLIE

This is a story around a new instalment in the reception of a medieval Irish text known as 'Buile Shuibne' or, in English, 'the madness (or fury) of Sweeney', elements of which are said to date back to the ninth century. The received version comes from about the early thirteenth century.[1] There's scarce an Irish poet or scholar who hasn't tried their hand at translating it, from Padraic Colum to John Kinsella, Patricia Monaghan to Greg Delanty, and, most famously, Seamus Heaney.

Without getting too entangled in the thicket, between Roman 'civitas' and pagan tradition, spear-points and psalter-retrieving otters, for present purposes, let's just say, Shuibne mac Cólmain Chúair, King of Dál nAraidi, has a curse laid on him by Saint Rónán. The saint has marked out the bounds of a church on Shuibne's turf and Shuibne is having none of it. But St Rónán (Rónán Finn mac Beraig: a conflation of Rónán Finn mac Sáráin of Colla Fochrích, associated with Magheralin, Co. Down, and Rónán mac Beraig of Uí Néill, abbot and patron of Dromiskin, Co. Louth) has the better of the confrontation. His curse drives Shuibne mad. In his madness, he deserts a battlefield and loses everything: his kingdom, his devoted wife, not least his regalia and raiment, and of course his right mind. It is in many ways a tale of the new Roman world order triumphing over the old. It is also an invaluable repository of medieval Irish poetry.

Transfigured into a bird-like creature, Shuibne flits hither and thither, stark naked, all across, around and beyond the island of Ireland, in great hardship, roosting in thorny trees and other discommodious wild spots, living off watercress, berries, nuts, but mostly watercress, lamenting his lot in vivid verses, and some fine nature poems. He also demonstrates a talent for 'leaping'. One of the places he finds himself in, in all his abject, bareforked, Lear-on-the-heath wretchedness is a ford on the Shannon, with a name in Irish that translates as 'Swim-two-birds'.

Many English-speaking readers of the postwar generation, like myself, quite probably had their first encounter with 'Sweeney', if they had one at all, in Flann O'Brien's *At Swim-Two-Birds* (1939). The wider comedy in O'Brien's method and his fine English-language renditions of Sweeney's Irish-language poems apart, we may all yet be forgiven for sympathising with O'Brien's 'Good Fairy' when at one point he says 'querulously': 'Put green moss in his mouth… are we going to spend the rest of our lives in this place listening to talk the like of that?'

If Shuibne's situation is Lear-like, his tales of woe also sound somewhat like Job, for whom no comfort or comforting will do. Not that Shakespeare or the Old Testament can have any bearing here. Nor is Shuibne without those who would comfort and help him out of his 'panic-lunacy', as Rody Gorman phrases it. But he won't be helped. On he flits and laments, bemoaning his plight. Some might think him monotonous, and it must be said, however entertainingly bizarre and wild and far-flung it is, *Buile Shuibne*, though by no means a work of great length, does have its longueurs. The 'Good Fairy' has a point.

But has O'Brien, the master of proportional representation, in his witty wisdom, spoilt us for a more direct approach to the original? Quite possibly. By 'us' I don't mean scholarly medievalists and Irish/Gaelic language authorities. They're another kettle of watercress altogether. But we of the *reader* species, genus now *Uncommon* and on the 'red list', and, sad to say, it seems, for the most part monoglot.

O'Brien's comic narrative and his skilfully composed verses leaven his source. There is no such leavening, no 'Good Fairy' commentary, in Seamus Heaney's recasting of the tale, in *Sweeney Astray* (1983), originally published as part of the Field Day project. No 'Good Fairy' and not really a 'Good Friday' dimension, if it's permissible to be so anachronistic and to look for hints of the Troubles in that way. The work reminds us of times when there was no 'Northern Ireland', for sure. It lends some support to the view of the Scottish Gaelic scholar Domhnall Stiùbhart that up to the founding of the Free State and partition, at least, Ireland might reasonably be considered the largest island in the Hebridean archipelago – a most enlivening perspective.

But any temptation to read Heaney's version as offering, in 1983, a breath of fresh air to the stifling atmosphere of the Troubles, through a momentary figurative uncoupling from 'Britishness', should be approached with caution. *Sweeney Astray* might be seen in such light if we so choose and it was clearly Heaney's intention that it should be. But *Buile Shuibne* itself certainly can't be. Indeed so much as a mention here of the 'Briton' or 'Britain' and 'Britishness' is most likely to lead us all astray.

When Shuibne travels beyond Ireland, he visits the island of Eigg in the Hebrides, and, notably, has an especially punishing stay on the Ailsa Craig (subsequently 'Paddy's Milestone', sometime Catholic haven), off the coast of Ayrshire, in the outer reaches of the Firth of

---

[1] The complex textual provenance of *Buile Shuibne* as we have it is traced by Máirin Ní Dhonnchadha in 'The Cult of St Molin and Buile Shuibne' (2013), published in *Buile Suibhne: Perspectives and Reassessments* (proceedings of the fifteenth annual seminar of the Irish Texts Society). This essay adopts the form 'Shuibne', the spelling given by CODECS (Collaborative Online Database and e-Resources for Celtic Studies).

Clyde. But when we hear (in Heaney's translation) that he has gone to the land of the Britons, this is to lead us into temptation. I would like to think that the reference to a mad Alan singing about a waterfall at Doovey (as given in Heaney) is to a Welshman at Aberdyfi, the Welsh being the ancient British in my book. But Gorman shows us that this is quite another madman (there's no shortage of them in his pages but none I think is Welsh). This one is 'mad Allan' from the great wood near Dumbarton Rock, who drowns at Essduich, or Duffy's Falls. Here we're in the speculative realm of Clach nam Breatann, which is something else, whatever it really amounts to, at the murkier end of our archipelagic history.[2]

Shuibne's plight doesn't provide anything near a coterminous analogy for the fate of Heaney, outcast from the North by the Troubles as he was (if not dethroned as head bard) and ever more wide-ranging spiritual wanderer, as he would become. This want of topical weight, as I see it, does seem to haunt *Sweeney Astray*. It's hard not to expect that weight from a poet whose gift for discovering analogy is generally astonishing. His rendition of *Beowulf* is better freighted and due North in this regard.

But writers aren't responsible for our expectations. Nor are non-contemporary works (medieval or otherwise) written to accommodate postscript interpolations, superimpositions, or ahistorical interpretations, and we should acknowledge and applaud their stubbornnesses, if they withstand our efforts to lay claim to them for our own ends. They were not written with us in mind. Anyone who triumphs over them nonetheless deserves high, and indeed *vide* 'The Odyssey' and James Joyce's *Ulysses*, the highest accolade, for, in this case, closing historical time down, into a visionary cultural moment of ironic renewal.

To take Seamus Heaney's more conventional line of flight further through the thorny branches, we must turn to Part III of *Station Island* (1984), 'Sweeney Redivivus'. Here the figure of Sweeney or the idea of him helps the poet articulate his own psychodrama, the conflicts involved in being an artist, and being from his 'home place', moving 'from a justified line / into the margin' to keep watch at his 'hidebound boundary tree', his 'airy listening post', sometimes 'like a scout at risk behind lines' and so on. In these poems Heaney's predicament as national poet blows and tugs through the poems with that sureness and obliquity of touch we associate with him at his best.

But 'Sweeney Redivivus' is not burdened by a demanding 'original' and an unstable one at that. It translates from the poet's mind only. Translation, it is commonplace to say, is an entirely other matter, between the poles of the literal – the austere, unforgiving principles and procedures, at work in Nabokov's Englishing of *Eugene Onegin*, for example – and imitation, in the manner of a Robert Lowell, or a Tom Paulin (a poet, indeed, with an interestingly asymmetrical relationship with Ulster; that is to say, somewhat astray). Heaney's approach is very much more in their direction.

As to the work of 'translating', as Heaney saw it, I once heard him remark to an audience that when he'd got on a roll with his version of *Beowulf*, much of the work, he said, was like turning a wheel; and he made a winding gesture, to show how he churned it out. There are fine moments in it and characteristic clarity of seeing, but, to my mind at least, a fair bit of churning seems to have gone on in the making of *Sweeney Astray*, more in the verse than the prose sections (which in the 'original' are suspected of being Christian scribal interpolations).

For his part, Gorman throws all this up in the air spectacularly. He deepens and enriches beyond words, or beyond words as we generally know them. As for words as we don't know them, I refer you once again to Flann O'Brien. That is, in the person of Myles na gCopaleen, as provoked by the pedantries of the lexicographer Patrick Dinneen. In the course of an *Irish Times* column or two on 'The Gaelic', Myles cites a lady lecturer on the Irish language who remarks that 'while the average English speaker gets along with a mere 400 words, the Irish-speaking peasant uses 4,000'. Myles's point is that the lady's figures are fallacious. '400/400,000 would be more like it,' he says; and further, 'In Donegal there are native speakers who know so many million words that it is a matter of pride with them never to use the same word twice in a life-time.' (One of the key commentaries on *Buile Shuibne*, by the way – dated 1629 in Gorman's footnote – was created by Micheal Ó Cléirigh: a scion of the Ó Cléirigh family of Donegal poet-scribes and chroniclers, and, as the architect of 'The Annals of the Four Masters', perhaps the most illustrious of them.)

Gorman is more of the Donegal class of Gael. His virtuosity within the Gaelic languages (and what is called *lingua gadelica* – the two forms of Gaelic in one) is dazzling (and highly humorous) and his scholarly engagement with the textual history of *Buile Shuibne*, not to say the history of Ireland, bettered I imagine by no one, though Sir Myles might beg to differ 'on principle', and others on particular points of fact. He energises his material with songs, haiku and 'round-trip' translations from Heaney and Joyce, present-day references, and not a longueur in sight (bad c[r]ess to the Good Fairy).

Now see him enter, formally, alighting from his roost on the Isle of Skye, at Sabhal Mòr Ostaig, and bearing a copy of his *Sweeney: An Intertonguing*,[3] a latter-day psalter for devotees of Gaelic studies, and speaking in tongues: Irish Gaelic, Scottish Gaelic and English.

'Intertonguing' is a literal translation of the Scottish Gaelic for 'translation': 'eadar-theangachadh'. I first observed it at work in poems Gorman sent me with a view to publication back in 2012. The poems fascinated me. So I took a couple of them, Gaelic original, with accompanying intertongued version, and published them in Issue 7 of *Archipelago* (Winter, 2012). Gorman had much more up his sleeve but my Press wasn't at that

---

2 Clach nam Breatann, a large megalith, said to have marked the boundary point between Dál Riada, Strathclyde, and Pictish territory to the northeast.
3 Published in 2024 by Francis Boutle Publishers of London, to finely judged production values.

time able to afford its publication in book form, which is what he sought, and the work required, to make full sense of it and his method.

Here's the intertongued opening stanza of one of the poems I took, one written 'for the Mackinnons', with a title that translates as 'In Cruard':

> I was inwombside it hourtime and hourtime. This vespersafternoon, as
> longfar as I remember, is when I found out the charactername they have
> for it, Herring Island. And that sea-clamwebspot uncovered at high tide
> over by beside it? That's the Àrdag, they said. News to me I said. And all
> those wells – the Well of the Richfoamcloudrelationbushbranchtrees, the
> High Well.

That the compounded words are Joycean in feel is immediately obvious. Just hear this, for example, as Leopold Bloom in the 'Circe' episode, reflects on a narrow escape, from a:

mangongwheeltracktrolleyglarejuggernaut

How would they say that in the Gaeltacht? Gorman would know. (He manages, incidentally, long after the demise of the Dublin United Tramway Company, to provide us with an encounter with its speedier successor, the *Luas* – Irish for speed – an encounter with which Bloom might well not have survived, thus changing our take on 16 June forever.)

Ulysses is one thing, *Finnegans Wake* another. Gorman's magnum opus, I suggest, aspires also to a grand 'chaosmos' model à la *Wake*. Either way, it is kaleidoscopic. It embraces all manner of reference, including Freemasonry's 'Great Artificer'. What would Shuibne have made of that, I wonder? – 'What's that bloody freemason doing...', he might have asked, 'prowling up and down outside?' – as the Citizen asks in the 'Cyclops' episode of *Ulysses* on catching sight of Bloom. Not that Freemasonry is an anomaly in a medieval context. It's just a tentacular anomaly beyond it.[4]

The 'Great Artificer' only has a mention in passing. He doesn't appear in Gorman's list of thirty-six 'Dramatis Personae' (where we may take it he is supplanted by 'God'), first among whom is: 'The Unstable Narrator', followed by 'Sweeney Gelt – deranged ex-king' and a host of kings, clerics, scribes, Saint Columba, various madmen, a hag, a madwoman, some 'Flax Women', 'Justmen', hoodlums, an altar boy, a church warden, a swineherd, wives, sisters, 'The Voice'.

The text leaps from language to language with the spring-heeled agility of Shuibne himself (in what Gorman at one point calls his 'Foolish Flickerflight'), and there is no doubt that some knowledge of Gaelic must be truly a great boon to the reader's pleasure in and understanding of this work. But it is far from essential, and readers without either form of Gaelic but curious to know more should certainly not be deterred from buying this finely produced book in which the 'intertongued' compound words come fast and if not quite furious *à la buile*, often hilarious – to my eye and ear, always 'Good Fairy' proof. There is little one can do to capture or evoke what goes on here in the wondrous thicket of Gorman's pages (indeed one should say his mind) but to quote him, by opening the book at random. As I have just done, at 'Chantsingcalltalking' (spellcheck now going at it mad as Shuibne himself):

> We heard chantsingcalltalking in the yew above us and the farewellcelebrationwarbling of the elkouzel from the regardpeak and humming and crycall of the Jovelordwoodbrown champion-stag and the croodleruckling of the gluttonbrawler, the tuftembracequaichbundlefalsetto cuckoo of the tuftembracequaichbundlefalsetto cuckoo of the Bann, the house crowd at a beerfest, the censurevoice of the whistleplover and the strings of humpharps however smallsmooth and there's no peaksweeter songmusic on earth.

And here, for a final example from well past the halfway 378pp mark, we come upon the very nub of the story, Saint Rónán's curse, a passage showing, incidentally, how method and madness flickerfly about in Gorman's unstable narrative, in a manner Flann O'Brien would surely have applauded:

> The pious cleric said... may he never have comfort or relief, or his familycommunity or the seed of his clanfollowerdescendants but to go fannelflutteringloitering and full-onfloathovering supportsuffering without food, without a drink of pureclean water, without heat, without a house, without help, without covering, without sleep ever again, without rest in fatesellrevange aboutunder God's testament-commandment.

---

4 For a brilliant account of Masonic matters as figured in *Ulysses* see Anne Marie D'Arcy, 'Joyce and the Twoheaded Octopus of Judéo-Maçonnerie', *Review of English Studies*, November 2013.

Poems

LAURA SCOTT

Table Talk

He stepped out of his self as if it were a lovely loose
dress you slide off shoulder by shoulder and drop

so it falls and pools around your ankles and you just step out.
He wanted to see what he looked like from the outside,

what they all looked like, sitting around the table, half drunk
bottles of wine all over it, plates pushed aside, long-handled spoons

balanced on the edge of low flat bowls and him, slightly slumped
back in his chair, forearms at oblique angles to his chest, palms turned

towards the ceiling – that's what he looked like, but what was he doing?
Holding court ? God, no, but the others were leaning in and some of them

even had their faces resting in the hammocks of their own hands.
All he was doing was talking about boredom, playing a game with it,

taking it and turning it on its head like a big beautiful hourglass
he placed in the middle of the table, showing them how, if they let themselves

sink into boredom's bluey grey waters (that's when he'd turned his palms)
they'd feel how it dragged time, slowed it down and down

until they could see (that's when they'd leant in) the coloured grains
of sand falling one by one through a nipped-in glass waist.

On reading and forgetting Coleridge

Like the rain that rills
clear and clean
down the sloping walls

of the hills your words
stream in and out of my head
lighting new paths

as they go
awakening capillaries
undulling nerve endings

so (for a moment) I see
what you saw –
see clear

through you
the bird's wings
and that walnut tree,

see how the light plays
with its leaves
or the baby sleeping

next to you by the fire,
hear the sound of that
the sound of that sleep

its *gentle breathings*,
feel you absorbing that,
breathing it in

and breathing it out
into your words,
the words I read

and pull into my lungs
until I hear it too
and remember the sound

of my own son breathing
as he slept in my arms
his ribcage moving

under my hand.
How do you thin and stretch
membranes like that?

Is there a kind of greed
that feeds your wide-eyed stare
so it spills out into us?

I don't know, but I love
the generosity of it,
the open-armed vulnerability

of giving like that,
of laying it out
like a wonderful lunch

on a table in the garden
under the trees
where you keep bringing

plate after plate
sprinkled with herbs
drizzled with oil

but still I read you greedily,
knowing, in a moment,
it'll all be gone.

Come live with me and be my love

said the tree to the sky
but before the sky could answer
the wind picked up

and for a moment the tree
let go its grip on the cool dark earth
and its roots came shrieking out

and the whole city of branch
and trunk, to say nothing
of the crows' nests so carefully woven

into its crown, came crashing down
and the sky looked at the orangey black
roots, out there in the open,

and turned its face away.
But something about the tree –
the unabashed way it spoke of love

maybe, or the familiar easy layout
of its line, the way *me* led to *my*
and *live* led to *love* like a branch

dividing with imperfect symmetry –
made the sky go back
and look again and this time

it saw leaves on fallen branches
moving like a shoal
of fish swimming

to stay still. And everywhere
the air was full of sounds and
the sky lived and loved them.

ants

they have a plan
and I don't know what it is

I hate all of them
all except one
over by the grass

who just watches
it grow.

Anthony Hecht's Prisoners of Time

ANDREW DICKINSON

It is rather strange to be speaking, but I know you are there

Reading through Anthony Hecht's recently published *Collected Poems* amply demonstrates that he wrote great poetry of many (and overlapping) kinds: lyrical ('Curriculum Vitae', 'Still Life'), narrative ('The Short End', '"More Light! More Light!"'), political ('Terms'), ekphrastic ('The Deodand'), satiric ('The Dover Bitch'), comic ('The Ghost in the Martini') and meditative ('Rites and Ceremonies'). Despite the excellence of these examples, Hecht's richest, most compelling and moving poetry may be his dramatic verse. Though early admirers (Harold Bloom and Christopher Ricks among them) stressed Hecht's achievement in the genre – comparing him, respectively, to Shakespeare and T.S. Eliot – recent critical opinion has turned. David Orr slights Hecht's 'speech-imitating creations' as 'talking dolls', while William Logan dismisses his 'strained personae' and 'humdrum people'. Even A.E. Stallings, in an admiring review, allows that among the 'barriers to Hecht's wider popularity' is his 'penchant for extended dramatic monologues'.

Hecht's successes in the genre include 'Green: An Epistle', 'See Naples and Die' and the superb 'Apprehensions', an unsettling poem of apprehensive and misapprehending childhood. But I want to focus on one kind of dramatic monologue which Hecht was a master of: the kind spoken by an attenuated, disappointed, belated speaker, who reminisces on and from a 'shipwrecked existence' (as Hecht says of Elizabeth Bishop's 'Crusoe in England'). These speakers are often approaching death and are driven to make one last-ditch effort to recall, confess or act. This kind of dramatic monologue, which might be termed the swan song monologue, has a rich history. Besides Bishop's 'Crusoe', examples include: Tennyson's 'Ulysses' and 'Tithonus', Robert Browning's 'Andrea del Sarto' and 'Childe Roland to the Dark Tower Came', Elizabeth Barrett Browning's 'The Runaway Slave at Pilgrim's Point', Amy Levy's 'A Minor Poet', John Leicester Warren's 'Philoctetes', Frost's 'The Witch of Coös', Pound's 'Exile's Letter', and Eliot's 'The Love Song of J. Alfred Prufrock' and 'Gerontion'.

Among Hecht's best examples of the subgenre are three poems he wrote in the voices of women: 'The Grapes' (1979), 'The Transparent Man' (1980) and 'Death the Whore' (1994). Each is written in blank verse, a form which Hecht said he used for the freedom it gave 'to move between an ordinary speaking voice and a voice of heightened poetic response to a moment'. In 'The Grapes', a hotel chambermaid has a vision of a dawn-light moving over a bunch of grapes in water, comparing this to light edging over 'clustered planets':

>   And I seemed to know
> In my blood the meaning of sidereal time
> And know my little life had somehow crested.
> There was nothing left for me now, nothing but
>   years.

In the movement from 'nothing' to 'nothing but years', Hecht hollows time of significance and purpose, making 'years' sound like a sentence to be endured. It is a moment analogous to Crusoe's parenthetical aside, in Bishop's poem, which quietly flips on its head the clichéd belief that 'giving years' is always preferable to 'taking' them:

> (And I'd have given years, or taken a few
> for any sort of kettle, of course.)

Hecht wrote about 'The Grapes': 'Once you begin to find yourself a prisoner of time, then you can see symbols of its constant movement everywhere, including on the surface of grapes' – and speakers who find themselves 'prisoner[s] of time' recur in Hecht's monologues.

'The Transparent Man' presents another 'prisoner of time': a woman, obliquely based on Flannery O'Connor, who is in hospital dying of leukaemia. This poem, like 'The Grapes', showcases Hecht's skilful movement between both an 'ordinary speaking voice' and 'a voice of heightened poetic response'. Hecht accepted Coleridge's injunction that 'a poem of any length neither can be, nor ought to be, all poetry'. But he also resisted the contemporary confessional style in which *none* of the poem was poetry, in which a whole monologue was restricted to what he called 'the unaffected and spontaneous speech of ordinary, unsophisticated people'. The speaker of 'The Transparent Man' is visited only by a Mrs Curtis, who brings a book-trolley to the ward each Sunday. Defending her father for not visiting, the speaker talks directly and colloquially:

>   It would take a callous man
> To come and stand around and watch me failing.

This draws its poignancy from being in small part true, but in large part untrue and overly forgiving (something that the line break after 'It would take a callous man' emphasises). The speaker later faces her fate with equanimity and a rising eloquence:

> But with leukemia things don't improve.
> It's like a sort of blizzard in the bloodstream

She is, like another of Hecht's speakers, a 'watcher at windows'. Looking out at trees in the barren landscape, she tries – before the 'sleeving snows' arrive – to understand 'how to deal / With such a thickness of particulars'. (This last phrase was borrowed by Jonathan F. Post for his excellent book on Hecht.)

In 'Death the Whore' a woman, dead by suicide, comes back to haunt a lover with insinuations and intimations of mortality (in this she resembles the terrifying monologuist of Beckett's *Eh Joe*). This last of Hecht's three women is a composite portrait of Sylvia Plath, Anne Sexton and another acquaintance of Hecht's who died by suicide. She is a 'prisoner of time' of a different sort. Apologising for her meandering, suggestive speech she says:

> As for my indirection, I'll just say
> I have more time than I know what to do with.

The monologue continues by 'indirection', slowly revealing a story of isolation, family betrayal and eventual death, with the speaker being cremated and 'thereby finding / More of oblivion than I'd even hoped for'.

Of all Hecht's monologues spoken by belated prisoners of time the best is 'The Venetian Vespers' (1978). It compares favourably to such great long poems of the 1970s as Ashbery's 'Self-Portrait in a Convex Mirror' and Merrill's 'The Book of Ephraim'. The poem condenses in its thirty pages the matter of a novel ten times that length. It is spoken by an expatriate American resident in Venice, a veteran medic of an infantry company discharged as 'mentally unsound'. Childless, financially supported by a dead uncle's inherited wealth, he is 'the tapered end of a long line', whose blood (in a beautiful play on the *circulatory* system) whispers to him 'on its nightly rounds'. He is haunted by memories of a sickly childhood's ominous inferences, belatedly revealed familial betrayals, wartime horror and interludes of insanity:

> My views are much like Fuseli's, who described
> His method thus: 'I first sits myself down.
> I then works myself up. Then I throws in
> My darks. And then I takes away my lights.'
> His nightmare was a great success, while mine
> Plays on the ceiling of my rented room
> Or on the bone concavity of my skull
> In the dark hours when I take away my lights.

The speaker is drawn again and again to the contents of that 'bone concavity'. We hear him say:

>   The mind at four AM
> Is a poor, blotched, vermiculated thing.
> I've seen it spilled like sweetbreads

And several pages later the memory alluded to here is described. A soldier in his company was shot in the head, revealing: 'His brains wet in the chalice of his skull'.

The poem is not solely occupied by 'the dark hours'; it is also an anthology of effects of light ('Lights. I have chosen Venice for its lights'). It contains some of Hecht's best descriptive writing: evocations of water, clouds, architecture and their mingling with light abound, which the speaker looks at intently and intensely:

> To give one's whole attention to such a sight
> Is a sort of blessedness. [...]
> One escapes from all the anguish of this world
> Into the refuge of the present tense.

If 'sight' is here depicted as one escape route from time's prison, the speaker goes on to doubt its efficacy. The poem's closing lines are powered by the speaker's despairing inability to echo Simone Weil's belief that 'looking is what saves us':

>   I look and look,
> As though I could be saved simply by looking –
> I, who have never earned my way, who am
> No better than a viral parasite,
> Or the lees of the Venetian underworld,
> Foolish and muddled in my later years,
> Who was never even at one time a wise child.

Besides the excellent notes amplified by its editor Philip Hoy from an earlier *Selected* (to which I owe the reference to Weil above), one of the riches of Hecht's new *Collected Poems* is its inclusion of the posthumous pamphlet *Interior Skies: Late Poems from Liguria*, as well as various uncollected poems. 'Menasseh ben Israel' from *Interior Skies* is another fine example of the belated dramatic monologue, recounting the Jewish scholar's voyage to England and his plea to Cromwell for the return of the Jews. It details his failed messianic mission and his posthumous existence after the death of his son: 'So in the end, in what was truly the end / Of everything'. Even better is 'Cain the Inventor of Death', presumably once meant for inclusion among the 'Presumptions of Death' section of *A Flight among the Tombs* (1996). As with many belated speakers of dramatic monologues, the poem begins in retrospection (unusually for Hecht, this is a monologue in rhyming quatrains):

> Gratefully I recall
> Ignited globes of dew
> The hilltop edged at dawn
> With sunlight's ormolu

This seems to be another speaker who, along with that of Hecht's short monologue 'Lot's Wife', might say: 'Who can resist the charms of retrospection?'. But then the picture darkens. 'Later a brother came':

> And once I hit him hard,
> Perhaps by some mistake,
> Hit him so that he slept
> And slept and didn't wake.

It's the line break at 'he slept / And slept' that chills.

Perhaps the best, and most novel, aspect of this volume is its accompanying audiobook. For this, Philip Hoy has gleaned several recordings of Hecht reading his own poems; Hoy himself reads the poems for which no such recording exists. Generally speaking, Hecht's best poems are read by Hecht himself (though 'The Deodand' and 'The Short End' are exceptions to this rule). Christopher Ricks notes that 'ghosts haunt Hecht's verse'. It is eerie to listen to Hecht voice his belated speakers from beyond the grave. And it is truly haunting to hear him speak 'A Voice at a Séance', one of his greatest monologues:

> It is rather strange to be speaking, but I know
>   you are there
> Wanting to know, as if it were worth knowing.

Listening to what Hecht's poems have to say, and how they say it, *is* worth knowing. More importantly, it is worth experiencing through the medium of Hecht's ghostly, resonant timbre.

Stilpo, late of Megara

EVAN JONES

Stilpo, once a citizen of Megara, about a half-hour drive from Athens, sought a life of tranquillity and had that taken from him. Demetrios Poliorkitis, by accounts a handsome and clever king, understood after he had conquered Megara that Stilpo – whom he regarded as significant – had suffered.

He summoned Stilpo and begged to restore his losses. But Stilpo, paraphrasing Homer, said no, no cattle or horses of his were stolen, no element of his education or any possession of his inner being was lost. How could it be? What Stilpo valued most, force and violence could not touch.

The Forum des Halles, Paris

1
Each farmer knew the land in Megara.
Holm oak, plane tree, alder.
Cecropian bees drank from the yew.
We threw the honey out. As a boy,
I was lost in the grove of Alkinoös,
daisies and grass, pale quinces.
The glade before they hacked
trees and went after Paris.
I was promised a small kingdom,
some safety from outside.
Soldiers came for us. Be death with me,
I said, here is the spot.
Five months' wading, coastguard,
cousins overseas. The tourist
who doesn't know what he wants
is welcome, the refugee who does less so.
One place led to many others.

2
I left monuments tacked
to the brickwork of rented space,
holdovers in place of memories
and real sensations, my grandmother
as a child, my grandfather
in his fishing jacket. I have his smile,
her sadness. Our ancestors
settled on life away from lack
and rifles. They abandoned
trauma and bored we threw
ourselves back into it.

3
Paris is half Parnassus,
half boulangerie, home of postcard
locales built of Lego and H&M.
At the intersection of Allées
Blaise Cendrars and Jules Supervielle
there is wealth those men couldn't know.
A display I take care to overlook.

4
By myself, misfiring in my habits,
what I mean is: no having and holding
of beauty if beauty is everywhere.
We can't live two lives at once,
feeding and clothing ourselves,
our children, pressed against
ambitions of, I guess, immortality.
Poetry thinks backward, forward,
drives everyone nuts or composes
them. Words themselves between
the leaf and the razorblade. Or neither.

5
The reason is, poetry named them both.

6
I condemn the times because I can,
just as through painting or sculpture
or the arches of Saint-Eustache,
we hold each other together.

7
We are asked to see the same thing:
the Eiffel Tower in Las Vegas,
the Parthenon in Nashville,
the Great Wall along the Mexican border,
now glowing, now rotten, troubling
the neighbours. Millennia of the same.
The sceptre of Phoroneus,
Decatur's conceit at Tripoli,
the disaster at Fukushima.

8
My mother with her mother and all
the houses they entered,
their children and work.
Long life ends at last and images
curl at the edges. I saw him,
King Demetrios, abrupt; he might've torn
the floorboards up himself.
Here you keep this roof beam,
there a table leg. His wealth
was worthless – not that I'm incorruptible.
He overspread. You can't commit
to lead and call it gold.
All my images of estrangement and fear
he created: the house still stands
but isn't mine. Away and far too much.

Everyone Loses Everything

The Poetry and Art of Meret Oppenheim

JENA SCHMITT

The Loveliest Vowel Empties: Collected Poems of Meret Oppenheim, translated by Kathleen Heil (World Poetry, 2023) £18.99; *Mein Album/My Album*, by Meret Oppenheim (Scheidegger & Spiess, 2022) £42

Meret Oppenheim (1913–1985) might be best known for *Object (Le Déjeuner en fourrure)*, 1936, a fur-lined cup, saucer and spoon that can be found in the Surrealist Objects gallery on the fifth floor of MoMA, alongside work by Leonora Carrington, Frida Kahlo, Alberto Giacometti, Man Ray, Picasso and Remedios Varo.

Rethinking these everyday objects, Oppenheim created an *objet d'art* at once decadent and playful, indulgent and feral, beautiful and unusable. Imagine trying to take a sip, lips pressed against the cup's lip. (Oppenheim pretends to do just that, in video footage, while setting up what would be her last exhibition, at Kunsthalle Bern, in 1984.) The furry service continues to provoke a delightful, some might say disgusting, synaesthetic response to art – the mouth feels dry just looking at it. But for Oppenheim it became something else: 'There is one thing I do not want you to ask', she said in 1978. 'I have been asked so often. "How did you have the idea of the fur cup?" It bores me'.

In other of Oppenheim's assemblages, white high heels are trussed together á la roast chicken and served on a silver platter (*Ma Gouvernante – My Nurse – Mein Kindermädchen*, 1936), wooden hands are manicured with red lacquer (*Fur Gloves with Wooden Fingers*, 1936), and laced leather boots connect amorphously at the toes (*The Couple*, 1956), making it impossible to take a step without falling.

Oppenheim also made drawings and paintings (*Angel of Death*; *Stone Woman*; *Red Head, Blue Body*; *Tous toujour*; *The Suffering of Genevieve*; *War and Peace*), collage (*Paradise Is Under the Ground*), furniture (a gilded table with bird's feet; a chair with a red tongue), performance art (*Spring Feast*, or *Frühlingsfest*), bronze sculpture (*Giacometti's Ear*; *Subterranean Bow*; *Six Clouds on a Bridge*), clothing and jewellery, including a wispy shredded-paper jacket, a sugar-cube ring, a set of stylish suede gloves handstitched with nerve endings, and bracelets covered in fur.

The Loveliest Vowel Empties, translated from the German and French by Kathleen Heil, is the first time that Oppenheim's poems have been collected in English. Here, the fur and stones and shoes and tongues abound in a fascinating dialogic exchange that visualizes the verbal and verbalizes the visual. Heil's translation of the title poem, 'The Loveliest Vowel Empties', refreshes the imagery Oppenheim worked with. This is also the title of one of Oppenheim's paintings: a blurry sphere connected to a chain that follows a long line of indistinguishable letters, perhaps a series of misshapen *O*'s that vocalize pleasure, or sorrow, or surprise, or pain.

In German, the three-line poem appears as:

Von Beeren nährt man sich
Mit dem Schuh verehrt man sich
Husch, husch, der schönste Vokal entleert sich.

The last line of the poem (and the title of the painting) has always been known as 'Quick, quick, the most beautiful vowel Is voiding', when referenced in galleries and publications. But Heil moves away from the falling flatness of the present participle *voiding* and its clinical connotation of bodily functions. Instead, she creates an active rush of movement and sound, space and air, the poem itself coming into being – breathing, building up, releasing:

> We feed on berries
> We worship with the shoe
> Whoosh! The loveliest vowel empties.

Heil's linguistic choices give the poem strength in translation, revitalizing it, making it active and new. And though she loses the nursery-rhyming *hush hush* (think 'Ring Around the Rosie', or trying to quieten a crying baby), she follows more closely the meaning of the word *entleeren* – 'to empty' – sliding the verb into the present tense. Connecting this with the metrically spacious *whoosh* makes sense, then, as though the word itself were emptying, in one long drawn-out syllable. If O is the loveliest vowel, there are now seven of them. In Oppenheim-like fashion, Heil ties the poem together.

In an another untitled poem, Oppenheim rewrites the legend – or is it a fairy tale? – of Geneviève de Brabant, who appears in the *Golden Legend* hagiographies of the twelfth century. When her husband arrives back from war and Geneviève is pregnant, he accuses her of adultery and sentences her to death. Her executioner takes pity, sends her into the woods to give birth and raise her child, where they nurse from a doe in order to stay alive. In Oppenheim's version:

> Everyone loses everything – as she, as ever
> Buzzed past in vain
>
> But:
>   Genevieve:
>
> Stiff
> Standing on her head
> Two meters above the ground
> Armless.
>
> Her son Schmerzereich:
> Unbearably swaddled in her hair.
>
> With her teeth she blows
> him off and away!
>
> Little fountain.
>
> I repeat: Little fountain.
> (Wind and shrieking in the distance.)

Schmerzereich ('deep pain'), the name she gives her son, reveals the conflict of motherhood, the limited choices Geneviève has to survive, the men who dictate those choices, the dependency and duty that bind mother and child together. At the same time, there is a ferocious, biting femininity here. Geneviève's teeth are bared; in one breath she protects her child, in another she could send her child away. Is her presence otherworldly – hovering above the ground on her head – or is it that she just has to work harder than the rest?

In her autobiography – published in *Mein Album*, part *Familienbuch*, part diary, part modern-day scrapbook that includes childhood drawings, photographs, notes and letters – Oppenheim explains in the third person her focus on Geneviève (Oppenheim herself is the *she* she refers to):

> She continues to work but few pieces survive. She is constantly blocked by periods of deep depression. A feeling of 'having her hands tied' – the drawing Geneviève (1942, a project for a sculpture) is like an illustration of her situation.

Both Oppenheim's writing and artwork speak to confinement – 'before, I was constrained. I wanted, couldn't, wanted, couldn't. I kept working, but without any contentment' – to synaesthetic sensations, to the dreamworld, and to the 'dual-sex spirit'. She often slips past expectations and constraints by setting traps, catching what she wants to catch, then letting go. In the prose poem 'As though awake while asleep seeing hearing', a man called Astor sees himself hearing, fastens his ears to a gnarled tree and falls asleep. When he wakes up, he finds in his pocket 'a calling card, printed with his new name: Caroline'.

As with the stories of Astor, Caroline and Geneviève, Oppenheim explores fantastical, fairy tale and mythological motifs. In the painting *Die Erlkönigin*, the therianthropic Erl Queen walks with a child in her arms, while in *Vogel mit Parasit*, a small white creature with wide eyes and pink ears sits atop a larger bird as they soar through the air. Both have set off on a journey, both are connected, parasitic, bound so tightly it is difficult to tell where one begins and the other ends. Who's to say where they are going and what they are leaving behind?

Everyone loses everything echoes throughout Oppenheim's body of work. She lived through both world wars, her family forced to leave Berlin for Switzerland because of her father's Jewish ancestry. They stayed in their summer house in Ticino, 'a beautiful old house, but without any comfort'. After joining her family in Switzerland from Paris when she ran out of money, Oppenheim had a small room above the garage and a space under the stairs for a makeshift kitchen. There was always a scarcity of supplies and resources, lack of money, a constant moving from place to place and a difficulty finding work. On top of that, there was isolation. In Paris, where 'night was turned into day', she had connected with a like-minded community of artists and writers including the Surrealists, and now that time was gone.

In the midst of war, there is always the everyday that needs attending to – meals to cook, rooms to clean, moments of stillness and beauty to find. In a handwritten note in French on hotel stationary from Padua, Italy:

> 1940 was a beautiful summer. I worked a lot in the garden, which distracted my thoughts a bit from the terrible war that was raging.

And later, after the death of her beloved grandmother:

> With great effort, I create a small garden in the little courtyard in front of my studio. Remove the paving, out with the bad soil, in with the new soil.

One can see in her poems a reflection of this work, references to gardens, flowers, stones, statues and insects. These instances are suddenly unsettled, turning quickly to decay and ruin: '[t]he daffodils quietly festered', 'lilacs blossom, lilacs flee', 'statues fall fainting to the earth', 'knives fly like birds through the air'. And in an untitled poem:

> Who thieves madness from the trees?
> Who have the heavens showered with hazy violets?
> How does one demise advise the next?

She writes in her autobiography about the anguish and uncertainty of war, where trenches '100 cm deep are dug in the square opposite the house in Rue Payenne' and 'how nobody could tell what would happen'. 'I'm expecting to lose everyone', she confesses, while in her poems there are soldiers' footsteps, Rottweilers, severed corpses, collapsing walls. Foxes eat their fur, the light is cleaved, there is not enough bread. The repetition is eerie, carnal, ominous:

> *I* gut my mushrooms
> *I* am the first guest come through
> And let fall the walls.

A different stanza is even more incantatory:

> The final word
> The final word
> Clasps its hands
> It sits on three chairs
> It makes a dense web of fallen words

Heil's English translations maintain Oppenheim's force as they move from language to language, from German and French (Oppenheim wrote in both), making determined, perceptive steps along the way. Heil keeps intact the *Komposita*, or compound words, that combine many nouns intricately together in German. Oppenheim invents many of her own, and the strange, unfamiliar word combinations create a revelatory effect in English. 'Fireworks pop and the night is sequinstrewn' gives a visual sensation of a star-riddled night sky. *Lebenslicht* is lifelight, *Rädermuse* is wheelmuse, *Schneeflockenmeer* is snowflakesea, and *Schneeflockenkammer* is snowquakechamber.

Oppenheim's inventiveness extends into vivid, pictorial lines – mauve waves, red meat, blue clover, yellow sky, black algae. Continuing the chatter between her poems and artwork, 'Your rhomboid face: rectangular, triangular, red-green / submerged in water. Amid the grass and all the rest, its sinking...' calls to mind the painting *Red Head, Blue Body* (*Roter Kopf, blauer Körper*, 1936). In another poem, 'dark figures', 'red embers' and 'blue-black grooves' mirror *Mourir la nuit* (1953), at Centre Pompidou, of a body rooted in the ground, a whirlwind of white swirls and scarlet flames flickering above.

Between 1937 and 1950, Oppenheim destroyed or left work unfinished, while some pieces went missing. She explains it as 'a crisis of self-confidence. The whole patriarchal world fell on my neck'. She notes in *Mein Album* that the painting *Quick, Quick, the Most Beautiful Vowel is Voiding* was lost in the war and recovered in a damaged state in 1981; *Tête de noyé, troisième état* (*Head of a Drowned Man, Third State*), writes Oppenheim, 'probably no longer exists'. Also:

> Ghost, painting destroyed
> Portrait destroyed
> Bird destroyed
> Cat destroyed
> 1941 destroyed
> Two Languages destroyed by me

In the last poem in *The Loveliest Vowel Empties*, 'Self-Portrait from 50,000 B.C. to X', which is also the last poem she wrote, she comes back to loss:

> ... My thoughts are shut away
> inside my head as in a beehive.
> I'll write them down later. The script was burned when the library at Alexandria burned. The black snake with the white head is located in the museum in Paris. It too will burn.

Today, at least, so much of Oppenheim's work remains – moments that have not yet vanished. There is the small painting *Steinfrau*, or *Stone Woman* (1938), reprinted in *Mein Album*, a woman made of stone slipping underwater; the crumpled blush-hued sheets in *Unmade Bed* (1939); a design for an 'evening suit', with buttons in the shape of plates and gold-embroidered cutlery. There is the black-and-white photo of Oppenheim as a child, beside which she writes in cursive – *In Deslberg, wearing the pretty red coat that I still remember*; an envelope addressed to Hotel Odessa; a letter from MoMA purchasing the fur cup, saucer and spoon for $50 in 1936; a note from Leonor Fini, about the heart-embossed gloves Oppenheim was to make for her – 'Can you call me before you leave?' Another, from Giacometti, written in French:

> Comment vas tu?
> Je te cherche et le telephone depuis 1000 ans.
>
> [How are you?
> I've been looking for you and calling you for
>   1000 years.]

And in *The Loveliest Vowel Empties*, there are the last four lines of the poem 'Self-Portrait', where the end is finally the end:

> ... The earth cracks, the
> spiritsphere bursts, thoughts disperse in the
> universe, where they on other stars
> live on.

Sonnets and 'The Returnee'

MARILYN HACKER

This used to be my daily pause-café,
bright, safe, if I came home at two AM.
I knew the waiters, and I greeted them
in French, Arabic, Portuguese, to say
the same things – 'Wretched weather !' or 'Nice day!'
I met friends here. I lived across the same
street, for months, then years, then a long time.
I'm killing time now, after a kiné
appointment, then the doctor, not till noon,
looking across the street at the front door
being painted turquoise! Where can harbor
be, if not here, where it was so long?
Café noisette, foam, and a tiny spoon.
Bathetic question... where do I belong ?

*

Dear Meg,
        Perhaps because I hadn't fallen
in love, or into bed, with anyone
the night before my transatlantic plane
flight, though I had my notebook open,
there was no drama or exchange, no ball in
the court to volley. I gnawed a Bic pen
and cursed the drought that parched imagination
dry. I love sunlight, but 'Send my roots rain!'
Cambridge, Massachusetts, bright Indian
summer: how bizarre, I haven't been
here for – six years? Neighborhood garden:
near a huge coleus, two gray-haired women
lean on their spades to chat. Gold flowers of autumn;
someone's tomatoes left to rot on the vine.

*

Dear X,
        Now we exchange letters by email,
and yours are extravagantly misspelled.
I'm older than I think I am. You're old,
too, my age plus nine. Can I still feel,
or just recall, the long emotional
downdrag of those years, until I hauled
myself back across an ocean? I never told
you: you came to see me one April?
August? in the troisième. Your hands
were so dirty, I was almost ashamed
to go to dinner with you. You work with books,
not water pipes or the innards of trucks.
Once, I desired you. Now, you were a man
who came with filthy hands to meet his 'ex'.

*

Dear Megan,
        When I was thirty-seven
I was the single mother of a six-
year-old, biracial and dyslexic.
I had three books – just one of them broke even.
I'd loved men. Now I was a lesbian,
as if desire were moved by politics,
as we self-mocked, 'politically correct',
but I heart-breakingly desired each woman
who broke my heart.
        Now I'm an old woman,
lame, with a cane, my sexuality
irrelevant. My daughter still can't spell,
but she's a doctor, living her difficult
life. Years passed, drained out, to what result?
I limp, or leap, to meet you at the table.

*

Dear X,
        Desire for you once filled a book,
that had two continents, two deaths, a child
wisecracking beyond her years in it, exiled
elders, some sex scenes, daybreaks, and the look
of a lover leaving, seen from the back:
blue jacket, scarf, blonde hair a little wild
in the rising wind that, hours ago, was mild.
And I took a notebook out of my backpack,
opened it on whatever surface was near,
like Berryman, girl gone, began to write
my shipwreck chronicle, all me, less you.
Now you're a businesswoman, sixty-two
(or something) with a wife. I'm sexless, 'queer'
politically. And when night falls, it's night.

*

All of the beds in which I couldn't sleep –
no, not because of making love, or yearning
for some lover, but lying awake till morning
in a sweat, a panic, in the grip
of repetitive worries, bugs that leap
from under mental floorboards. My head's burning.
My feet are cold. And when did I cease learning
to deal with my surroundings, to escape
anxiety in rhymes, verb conjugation,
in camomile tea, in masturbation
to a suitably improbable fantasy?
I don't knock myself out with medication
as some insomniacs, desperate as I,
have done. But want sleep before the next day.

*

All my possessions stacked against the wall
in cardboard boxes that I didn't pack –
as if they knew I wouldn't be coming back,
the student tenants who disposed of all
I owned, emptied the armoire, filled the hall
with my books in more boxes, and my stack
of dictionaries, English, French, Arabic.
They're gone, but how to reconstruct, recall,
revivify 'the life that once I led',
from which I ignominiously fled?
I talk to the waiters, the desk-clerk
in all the languages of solitude,
and try to do what I think of as work.
On a 'device', Noor, Layla, wounded, dead.

The Returnee
العائد

'There is no surah of *The Returnee*',
he writes. 'Bombs blew out the bathroom door,'
she writes, 'but nobody was in the bathroom,
hamdulillah. We are waiting for more news.'

He writes, 'Bombs blew out the front doors
and windows of all the buildings on the street.
'Thank God, we had a little more news
from my aunt and uncle. They're well, if you call it "well".

No windows in all the buildings on the street.
'My little cousin cries, and hides her tears
from my aunt and uncle. They're well, if you call it
   "well".'
She stares as if her gaze would keep them safe.'

'My little cousin cries, and doesn't sleep.
She wants to go to school, and see her friends,
as if her gaze somehow would keep them safe –
play hide-and-seek, read out loud together, recite.'

He wants to go to school and see his friends,
recognise their faces, say their names,
play football, read out loud together, recite
a surah, a poem – even make one up.

Recognise their faces, say their names...
Sometimes it eases tension to recite
a surah, a poem, even make one up
if the text you need doesn't exist.

Sometimes it eases tension to recite
what you wrote down last night, by candlelight.
If the text you need doesn't exist
you make it up. Resistance, old words, worth repeating,

you wrote last night under fluorescent light.
Is it inevitable that sons and daughters
of the Book (which book, they all exist?)
and of exile send others into exile?

Inevitably, I'm a granddaughter of refugees,
welcome, then, as inexpensive labour,
exiles who sent no one into exile,
shopkeeper, factory girl, bookkeeper,

welcomed, then, as inexpensive labour.
Some of their sons and daughters went to college,
children of factory workers and shopkeepers.
Murder continued, altogether elsewhere.

Some of these sons and daughters would have studied
medicine, languages, literature.
They were murdered, in Gaza, elsewhere,
fire from the sky, breath snuffed out under rubble.

Language as medicine? Literature
as ceasefire? Maybe when/if it's over,
fire from the sky snuffed out, some of the rubble
lifted, and a survivor emerges.

During a pause in the bombing, pause nearly over,
some women shoulder a slab of fallen stone,
lift it, and a survivor emerges.
Whose Issa[1] is he, what can he redeem?

'Some women shouldered a slab of fallen stone,'
he wrote, 'but no one alive was underneath.'
No Issa rising to proclaim good news.
There is no surah of *The Returnee*.[2]

---

1 'Issa' is 'Jesus' in Arabic. As in Spanish, it is a common name, for Muslims and Christians alike.
2 The idea of a – non-existent – Quranic surah entitled *The Returnee* came from an essay by the Palestinian American poet Fady Joudah.

Feedback Noise

IAIN BAMFORTH

It is 2 December 1917, a year after the death of the Emperor Franz Joseph. His was a reign that lasted almost seventy years and became a byword for stability in central Europe much as Queen Victoria's did in the English-speaking world. In one of the Empire's provincial capitals, Dr Franz Kafka, an accident insurance specialist, writes a starveling fable in what is now known as the *Blue Octavo Notebook*. It spells out a concise metaphysics of mass-mediated communications.

'They were given the choice of becoming kings or regal messengers. The way children are, they all wanted to be messengers. That's why there are more and more messengers hotfooting across the world and proclaiming, in the absence of kings, messages to each other that have become meaningless. They would like to put an end to their miserable lives but dare not because of their oath of service.'

The final sentence darkens the perfect image of 'little angels' unhappy at having made an ostensive declaration of fidelity to the imperial courier business. In Kafka's fable, the vocation of being regal envoys or emissaries has displaced all the others. It's the only game in town. If exchange is fundamental to human flourishing, these children's singular choice was right on the money. Lots of messengers whizzing around suggests a wealthy realm: power is the ability to control a territory though messages – read transport and transmission.

But where are the layers of society between kings and their subjects? Kings are important persons, they *importune*. They need mediators. So where are they? The absence of kings cries out from its parenthetical phrase ('da es keine Könige gibt'): this little tale begs to be read as a reflexively negative theology, in which the unquestioned singular authority that undergirds the structure can't represent or fully account for its own not being there. Clearly something calamitous has happened to the compact of the body politic. It takes a traditionalist like John Ruskin – who remembers and feels no shame about the child within him – to admit to 'a most sincere love of kings, and dislike of everybody who attempted to disobey them'. Which is a way of saying that he understood kingship to participate in the divine. 'There's such a divinity that doth hedge a king', as Hamlet said.

For if kings don't exist some kind of higher instance must. Who condescended to offer these messengers a choice of career, and summoned them to hear their oaths of service? They have taken vows; they have *professed*. And they regard these vows as binding. To break them would be to break faith with themselves, a weightier kind of obligation than the social contract that governs so many powerful modern ideas from autonomy to self-interest.

And why have these regal proclamations become meaningless? Why do these juvenile communicants mouth empty utterances to each other? Because they're caught squabbling in the web of a system in which everything is immanent – who needs angels when everybody has a smartphone? The kings, the sovereign senders, those who traditionally command the space of attention in the theological and political sphere, no longer exist to make their messages authoritative. The Talmud says God never dispatches His messengers with more than one message at a time: Kafka invites us to consider that verticality can't develop precisely because these messengers are all looped into the same system, simply doing the rounds in a zero-sum game.

Children don't want to become kings because kings have the aura of the sacred about them, something frightful. Yet being absent from the scene is a compromising position for kings. A palace scandal, you might think, except that no palace exists to be scandalised. And come to think of it, what do kings really know about communications? – They don't even open doors.

In previous times, messengers were go-betweens whose work allowed the commandments of those highest authorities not to remain trapped in enigma. Messengers moved in a ready-made framework. Where there were distant places there had to be a centre from which such places could first be identified as lying on the outskirts. Messengers fly. They are centrifugal. As centrifugal as a liberal society, where sovereignty is dispersed. The circle expands, yet its radii all lead back to the notion of a centre (subject to endless revision).

And these errant children do all this in earshot of the absent kings to whom they once took an oath of fealty. They promise to pass on a tradition they don't understand. One as solemn as it is absurd. For all that their intentions are pure and their commitment steadfast they know themselves to be acting in bad faith. They want to be members of a social order which their original decision has revealed them as unsuited to join. Those living after the age of kings live in the knowledge of being unhappily communing agents of well-nigh unintelligible laws for the sake of peace among the nations: the generality of the rule turns out to be more intransigent than the instance it governs.

It seems to me these children pop up elsewhere in Kafka's work, at a crucial early juncture of his novel *The Castle* when the 'land surveyor' K. takes shelter in the village inn and seeks instruction from the authorities by telephone, eager to clarify why he has been summoned. K. picks up the phone and listens, without saying a word. 'From the earpiece came a humming of a kind K. had never heard on the telephone before. It was like the humming of countless childish voices – but it wasn't humming either, it was singing, the singing of very distant, infinitely distant voices – blended by sheer impossibility into one shrill yet forceful voice that was now drumming on the ear as if trying to penetrate beyond mere hearing.'

Not quite a message, this singing sound is made up of high-pitched childish voices, an untold number of them, mingled into one commanding high sovereign utterance, a kind of vocal bare life that overwhelms the spellbound K. This is the Castle's answer to his request, and it gets past his principal line of defence: his hearing. It is the first in K.'s successive misunderstandings of what those in authority intend for him. 'I don't want any act of favour from the Castle, but my rights', says K.

Which is something you can imagine those youthful bearers of empty tidings also demanding. If only they weren't quite so obviously and helplessly members of one another.

Four Poems
GREGORY WOODS

Nightfall in an Eyeball of Howard Hodgkin
i.m. Clare MacDonald Shaw

A sun like a tomato, juicy and nutritious,

when chopped by the serrated sierra, dispenses
a barrel of tarry darkness, sudden and sullen,
as if a vigorous heart were to be caught seething
with the bitterest of jealous thoughts, like black beetles;

and within a few minutes the temperature plummets,
leaping two seasons, so that when the moon has risen,
not half an hour later, it is already winter
and the day's sunbathers are putting on their woollies,

ruefully swapping reminiscences of summer.

Fire and Ice

The burning ships have been abandoned,
left to snuff themselves out overnight.
The Queen is in her cups,
not in any mood to lionize the heroes
or comfort their hysterical sidekicks.
In her tent on the clifftop
she orders her Chamberlain
to silence the fretful elements
and not to come back without a captive –
chieftain or elephant, something rare
and suitably subdued.
                    The rest of us,
the indistinguishable comradeship,
fused as if by fire and fixed as if by ice,
sit thoughtless on the bloody beach,
our eyes as empty of each other as
of what we came for: beauty, booty, and
that sense of manhood satisfied
we so despised and envied in our toothless fathers.

Scenes from Genet

1. Night had fallen.
   We arrived in a mass of shadows.
   We got out.
   Eight screws were in attendance
   in a line
   like footmen on the lighted steps.

2. It was absurd to put slang words and expressions
   in quotation marks
   since that hinders their entering the language.

3. I was sixteen, the age of young girls...
   Fifteen is slender
   and seventeen too hard,
   but sixteen has the ring of a delicate femininity.

4. His voice isn't
   – as is sometimes the case –
   tacked onto him
   but is made of the same solid matter as his body
   and the design of the gestures I felt so much a part of
   that I find it impossible to distinguish them.

5. Strong in their grace,
   so loftily did they wear
   their having-been-fucked
       it became
   both adornment and force.

6. When a child first discovers black lace
   he sustains a shock, a mild wound.
   He is stunned to learn that lace,
   the flimsiest of fabrics,
   can be an ornament of mourning.

7. Everyone has chosen (not on purpose
   but by some obscure process) a phrase
   that visits his lips more insistently

   and this phrase or formula
   takes the place of a device.
   It does what the prison bigshots' tattoos do.

8. He didn't love me. I loved him.
   In short: he was the demon inciting me
   to *more* toughness, *more* audacity, *more* love.
   Bulkaen was my virility.

9. More objectivity
   more passivity
   more indifference

   hence poetry

PS

Sudden loss of cabin pressure
Minutes to live
The manuscript in the overhead locker
The only copy
Reads itself for the last time
Committing to oblivion
All its indiscretions

Nothing will survive of us
We were individuals
Without as much value
As our passwords
And the rare metals in our devices

AI in the crashproof box
Think of us from time to time

From *What Is Poetry?*

PHILIP TERRY

In his *Observations on the Art of English Poesie* (1602), Thomas Campion makes one of the rare attacks on rhyme in the history of English poetics. Referring to the widespread use of rhyme in his day, Campion observes that 'things naturally imperfect can not be perfected by use' and concludes 'that ill uses are to be abolisht'. Rhyme, for Campion, frequently distorts the writing of many poets: 'it enforceth a man oftentimes to abjure his matter, and extend a short conceit beyond all bounds of art'. Another problem with rhyme, for Campion, is that it leads to 'a continual repetition of that Rhetoricall figure which we tearme *similiter desinentia*' which should be used sparingly 'least it should offend the eare with tedious affectation'. What Campion hints at here is the way that rhyme, in addition to distorting the writer's subject matter *for the writer*, distorts the reader's access to this matter, caught up as they are in the continuing jingle of the rhymes, to the point where they hear nothing else, and are thereby rendered deaf to everything except this mechanical music, a point made more recently by Tom Raworth. It's what made reading W.H. Auden difficult for me for years, until I developed a method of ignoring the rhyme. History, by and large, has ignored Campion – rhyming has remained the dominant tradition – but if he'd been listened to, the history of poetry in English would look very different: there'd be no Larkin, no Hardy, no Edward Thomas, little Auden, no Plath, no Porter, no Maxwell, no Armitage, no Ayres, no performance poetry. What the landscape might have looked like without these major landmarks, we can only guess.

*

A book on poetry made up of essays on fictional books of poetry.

*

Poetry and buildings. Without ever having consciously sought it out, occasionally I come across poetry on buildings: there's John Donne's 'The Sunne Rising' on the wall of Derek Jarman's Prospect Cottage at Dungeness, there are some stunning wall poems scattered across Leiden in the Netherlands, including work by Pierre Reverdy, Robert Frost and Marina Tsvetaeva, there are Angry Dan's limerick murals near Liverpool Street, and a poem by Andrew Motion on a student building in the centre of Sheffield, which I've seen when driving past in a car looking for somewhere to park, and about which the poet Alan Halsey wrote: 'It's said that Sheffield paid Motion / an unspeakable number of thousand pounds / for one of the world's worst poems'. And I've come across such poems in books, too, most recently Robert Fitterman's *Poems for Buildings*. Wall poems fall into two types, the out of the archive (Prospect Cottage; Leiden) and the made to measure (Angry Dan; Andrew Motion). Fitterman's are made to measure, minimalist, and composed with public display in mind, particularly the modern office space, as he explains in his introduction: '*Poems for Buildings* asks the reader to visualise these poems engraved into the marble wall of a lobby, appearing on an object in a building courtyard, writ large as a banner in an employee cafeteria, projected on hallway monitors etc. Because contemporary poetry rarely has the opportunity for public display, *Poems for Buildings* calls upon the reader's imagination to locate these poems off the page and onto office spaces, much like public art.' Unusually, Fitterman considers the *inside* of buildings as well as the outside, and his invitation to the reader to think of an ideal location for each poem makes the project a playfully collaborative one between writer and reader. Some of the poems reference the office environment in which they could be placed, and would sit well in a meeting room: 'who gets to decide / who gets to decide?' Others are slyly self-referential, and might sit well in a cafe: 'you might prefer a picture and you / wouldn't be alone'. Others call out for a toilet wall, or an outside space: 'what did I come here / to get / away from?' Others might work in an untidy work environment, like shared and overcrowded offices, elevating the infra-ordinary of the office into the realm of art: 'an empty shoebox on the floor for- / ever'. Others are just weirdly enigmatic – like 'even dollar oysters' – but taken as a whole the poems are a delight, and they bring something new to the idea of public poetry: they are not just 'poems' that could be put on (or in) 'buildings', they are poems designed specifically *for* buildings, bringing their meanings to and taking their meanings out of that very context, as if the building itself was an extension of the poem.

*

Concrete poetry is not a visual but a silent poetry.

Concrete poetry was considered childish because it was seen and not heard.

The Muse of concrete poetry reversed Mnemosyne's gift; depriving the poet of song, she gave him sweet eyesight.

(Ian Hamilton Finlay)

*

Found poetry. One time I remember talking about found poetry, though it was not the first time, was with the poet John Daniel – my Head of Department at the University of Plymouth – in Totnes. John proudly told me that he had once read from a telephone directory at a reading, and that he was the inventor of found poetry. I smiled, and probably laughed, but I was sceptical, thinking that found poetry had a history that stretched back to Dada at the very least, and was contemporaneous with Marcel Duchamp's experiments with found objects, from the *Bottle Rack* (1914) to the Mutt urinal, *Fountain* (1917). Just as anything can be art if you put it in a gallery – a light bulb, a pile of books, a decomposing cabbage, a dead shark – so anything can be a poem if you put it between the covers of a book of poetry, as conceptualists and uncreative writers have been doing ever since. I think I first tried out the found poem myself in my *Oulipoems*, a book I wrote in a fit of unconstrained pleasure and invention when it finally dawned on me that my brand of experimental novel was never going to find a firm foothold in the UK book market. For one poem I took an image of a speed camera, pointed it upwards, and gave it the title 'The Birds Are Flying Too Fast'. I returned to the idea in *Oulipoems 2* with the poem 'Birds of Joyce's Marsh', which consisted of an alphabetical list of birds to be found on Joyce's Marsh in Essex – beginning with Brent goose and ending with Yellowhammer – which I had taken down from an information panel. I've always seen the found poem, at its best, as like the objects in boxes by Joseph Beuys: just as Beuys makes you look at an everyday object again by putting it in a glass box, so the found poem makes you look at an idea or a word or a letter again by presenting it as a poem. In this sense the single letter and single word poems of the Oulipo can be seen as part of the tradition of found poetry. Other examples closer to home can be found in the work of Edwin Morgan, who triumphantly returns to the form in his collection *Newspoems*: here, typically, he cuts out found text from newspapers, then repurposes it with a title, so 'Meter eater' is given the title 'Car Goes Ape', 'HALT COMMIT ADULTERY' is given the title 'Notice in Hell'. And you can come across found poetry in unexpected places too, in the work of poets you didn't think of as found poetry poets at all, as I did recently in the pages of John Ashbery and Joe Brainard's *The Vermont Notebook* – was it the influence of Brainard? – like this:

> Prior to the artificial reefs, studies revealed that one fish could be
> caught for every two hours of fishing effort. Right now fishermen are
> averaging between seven and eight fish per hour, and sometimes the
> count goes up to 15 fish per hour. Divers from the Station have recorded 87 different species of fish on the reefs, with the most numerous sport species being groupers and jacks.

*

We ought perhaps to conclude that the language of today must have certain things in common with poetry, and that the two should sustain each other in both form and substance. In the course of daily life this relationship often passes unnoticed. Headlines, slogans, groups of sounds and letters give rise to forms which could be models for a new poetry, just waiting to be taken up for meaningful use.

(Eugen Gomringer)

*

Jonson was *the* poet to emulate: he serves the language, he does not inscribe it with his 'own character' or weave it in accordance with personal myth. The most classical of poets, he nourished himself on the classics and imparted classical virtues. His 'school', 'tribe', and 'sons' affirm something as salutary as it is strange to our age when poets are required to have 'a voice'. He and his followers were masters, with meanings to convey. In their art there is an element little valued now: self-effacement before the rigours of form and the challenge of subject.

(Michael Schmidt)

*

Imagine a bookmark, not one that you've bought or been given free with a purchase or found in a Christmas cracker, but one torn hastily from a scrap of paper or a newspaper to mark your place in a book before you lose it as you rush to answer your phone. It's not rectangular, but has a jagged edge, and a pointed or a sloped top, it's irregular. Now imagine it in a book: the top part that sticks out beyond the upper edge of the book will look like the outline of a mountain peak, or a small plateau, or some cliffs seen from out at sea. Now imagine this shape printed on paper, alongside other similar shapes, in outline, black on white, or blocked out in black ink, alternately. The shapes are arranged in eight rows... I'm describing, or trying to describe, a piece by Joe Devlin, published by the Swedish press Timglaset, who specialise in visual poetries. It's printed in an edition of ninety-nine copies and entitled *A Taxonomy of Protruding Bookmarks*. I've been picking this up and looking at it every evening for the past month or so, and trying to work out how to read it. If it's a poem, what kind of poem is it? I can read it as a visual poem, a series of images of protruding bookmarks, that, like Wittgenstein's Duck-Rabbit, also resemble something else, mountains or cliffs or a landscape. Or I can take it, as its title suggests, as a comment on taxonomy – you can imagine the protruding bookmarks kept in a museum drawer – either ironic, pointing to the impossibility of categorising everything, or marking the beginnings of a sincere attempt to categorise the surprising variety of shapes that might be adopted by protruding bookmarks, in the same way as Marcel Duchamp's *3 Standard Stoppages* shows us the various shapes that a falling one-metre-length of thread can land in. In this, the piece would resemble many poems – like those of Francis Ponge – that attempt to make us look at marginal and perhaps neglected everyday objects. The piece, in a word, 'makes strange' the bookmark. At the same time as it makes sense to read this as a visual poem, or visual piece, it has something that most visual poems don't have, but that we are used to in conventional poetry, and that is *lines*. The protruding bookmarks are arranged in eight lines, like a stanza, or the commencing octet of a sonnet, preceding the volta; and each line contains between seven and nine protruding bookmarks depending on their size, just as a line of conventional poetry – iambic pentameter, say – might contain between seven and nine words, depending on their length. Looked at from this angle, the piece resembles a curtal sonnet in its form, though it would be difficult to attach any precise meaning to it beyond that. You couldn't say with much confidence whether it's a love sonnet, or a holy sonnet, or a descriptive sonnet, though if you were going to push at one of these doors it might be the third, given the resemblance of the shapes to landscapes. As I continue to look at it from this point of view, as a part sonnet, I begin to see all of a sudden that it shows us not just images of fragments of bookmarks, but that it resembles, overall, a fragment of a larger text, and this in turn suggests how the whole might be seen – because of its undecipherability – as a fragment of a text from a lost language, whose code, embedded in each shape, is yet to be cracked. Like a fragment of *Gilgamesh*, written in cuneiform and glimpsed on a broken stone tablet, taking us back to the moment of the first encounter with this strange and foreign script when George Smith, visiting the British Museum in his lunch hour to peer at the flood tablets, slowly began to work out how to *read* them. There is a brief glimpse here, too, of a vast unread library, now lost, buried beneath the sands, tantalisingly and forever out of sight and out of reach. It's a glimpse that seems to take us a long way from where we started, but which paradoxically returns us to the origins of Devlin's piece, the library of now unrecoverable books – sixty-five in all – that these protruding bookmarks were originally placed in, the only remaining record of which is now this enigmatic taxonomy of protruding bookmarks.

*

if you dribble past five defenders, it isn't called sheer prose

(Tom Leonard)

*

According to the legend, bpNichol had been reading in the UK – he'd come over for the 8th International Sound Poetry Festival in London and he'd wanted to read from his poem 'Translating Apollinaire', an eccentric and impressionistic experimental translation of Apollinaire's 'Zone', but he couldn't as he'd left it in Toronto. Frustrated, en route from London to Toronto on 27 May 1975, in the company of Gerry Gilbert, he set about reconstructing the poem from memory. He wrote three versions, the first in the order in which he recalled it; the second rearranging that to achieve something closer to the actual order of the translation as he recalled it; the third, taking the first memory poem, and treating this as the first draft of a new poem, and revising. These three versions he referred to as 'Translating Translating Apollinaire 1', 'Translating Translating Apollinaire 2' and 'Translating Translating Apollinaire 3', or 'TTA 1', 'TTA 2' and 'TTA 3'. Here's 'TTA 1: memory translation (order of recall)':

flat on my back on the floor
becoming aware of it
                          for an instant

'soleil cou coupé'
rolls thru my window

sun thru trees passing
a million new wave movies

driving thru the city

The original translation, which he now renamed 'TTA 4', had already been an eccentric translation of Apollinaire – it is much curtailed, removing Apollinaire's reference to the modernity of Christianity and to refugees in Paris, and concentrating on the images of flight and the sun, while bringing more up to date fields of reference, such as new wave films, into play. This memory version, however, now radically curtailed and reordered, verges on being a new poem altogether, and as such marks an inaugural moment, perhaps *the* inaugural moment, in the history of experimental translation. As the series continued to grow and proliferate, Nichol added visual versions, versions which rearranged the letters alphabetically, versions which rearranged the poem according to word length or replaced words with their synonyms taken from *Roget's Thesaurus*, versions that treated each letter as the first letter in a new word (something he called 'acrostic' translation), sound versions, perambulatory versions regarding the translation from 'different sides', and so on. Many of the methods are of Nichol's own invention, others, by accident or design, bear some resemblance to the transformatory techniques of the Oulipo, which had been founded in 1960, when Nichol was sixteen, as they do to the variations in Raymond Queneau's *Exercises in Style*, which first appeared in English translation in 1958, when Nichol was fourteen. This was published by Gaberbocchus Press, run by Stefan Themerson, a Polish refugee, soldier, avant-gardist, translator and film-maker. Themerson himself – and it's not impossible that he was present at the 8th International Sound Poetry Festival, based as he was in London, and interested as he was in sound poetry (his close neighbour was the sound poet Bob Cobbing) – may also have had a seminal and unacknowledged influence on bpNichol, for his novel *Bayamus and the Theatre of Semantic Poetry*, published by Gaberbocchus in 1965, itself proposes an early method of experimental translation. He called this 'semantic poetry' and, not unlike the Oulipian method of definitional literature or LSD (*Littérature Semo-Définitionelle*), it consists of translating a poem by substituting *definitions* of words for the words themselves. So in Themerson's hands, the opening words in the Chinese poem 'Drinking Under the Moon' by Li Po becomes:

> The fermented
> > grape-
> > > juice
> > among the reproductive
> > > parts
> > > > of
> > > > > seed-plants

Which bears a striking resemblance to Nichol's 'TTA 19: replacing words in poems with their meanings using Webster's *Dictionary for Everyday Use*', which begins:

> Icharrus furnished with wings, enabling him to fly or hasten (wounded in the wing, arm or shoulder) to or toward a higher place or degree; Simon the one skilled in magic (a conjuror), out of Judea, elevated far up indicating a present relation to time, space, condition, the indefinite article, meaning one perennial plant having trunk, bole, or woody stem with branches; all possible people stretching out their hands, straining after a conception, or to denote a particular person or luminous body round which earth and the other planets revolve.

*

In her collection *breath:e st(utter)ance* (2023), Rachel Smith develops a method of notating a reading process: in particular the way that, as readers, our attention drifts, how we misread, misconstrue punctuation and bring in irrelevant associations. As she puts it: 'It takes delight in the generative properties of error'. Punctuation, she notes, draws attention to the rhythm of breathing, but it also acknowledges the moments of distraction and association while reading. The work takes Gilles Deleuze's book *Logic of Sense* as reading material to explore this process, quoting and deforming Deleuze as she proceeds, sometimes by association, sometimes by poetic deformation, sometimes by use of autocorrect. So 'breath' metamorphoses to 'breathe' then to 'brea(d)th'; 'utter' hovers between 'stutter', 'utterance', 'utter(st)ance' and 'stance'. Each page is further subject to deformation and distraction and drift by being printed on transparent vellum, so that we get a glimpse into the pages that are coming: behind each word, on other pages, we can see rectilinear grids which highlight and enclose certain words or stand stubbornly on their own, suggesting architect's plans; giant punctuation marks which seem to drift off from the text into a nascent and detached world of visual poetry where commas might be tadpoles, stops great balls, or, enlarged further, planets; other pages are covered with smoke-like traces of ink as in an erased and indecipherable manuscript, or like the thoughts of the dreaming reader, or the smoke of a cigarette they have just lit as they sit at their desk. Sense drifts like smoke: 'I am lost // lost : list : lust // lostness becomes the unintended destination'.

In *Logic of Sense*, Deleuze unsettles our notions of sense via a series of paradoxes. Sense is itself constituted through difference – associations, wordplay, accident – and is always imbricated with its apparent opposite, nonsense, which like the unconscious threatens to disrupt its apparent continuities. At the heart of *breath:e st(utter)ance* Smith gathers together an extensive list of paradoxical Deleuzian definitions of sense, all of which aim to unsettle its authority, including:

> *Sense is always a double sense*
> *sense is not 'sense'*
> *sense, [...] is doubly generative*
> *Sense is always an effect*
> *Sense is that which is formed and deployed at the surface*
> *Sense is actually produced*
> *Sense is never only one*

In Smith's treatment, Deleuze's text itself is subject to disruptive deformations of sense, as the word 'sense' itself metamorphoses into 'since' and 'scents' and the punning 'resent', which in turn takes us to a word chain that includes 'present', 'pursuant', 'presentation' and 'preservation', all of which, particularly the binaries 'present' and 'pursuant', suggest alternatively the presentness and the non-presentness of language and meaning. At times meaning threatens to disappear altogether, to fall into a void – [...] – as the text is as if invaded by its punctuation, which threatens to take over, as in a nonsense novel about a revolution of punctuation marks which start growing and never stop, overtaking all the white space on the page, *Alice in Punctuationland*. Here, perhaps, we glimpse a nightmare world in which nobody can articulate anything at all, where we are lost in a world of infinite regression of meaning, as in the darker moments of *Finnegans Wake*. It is a world hinted at in *Alice Through the Looking Glass* (the text is quoted at length by Smith), where in response to the Red Queen's dictum 'Speak when you're spoken to!' Alice responds by saying: 'if you only spoke when you are spoken to, and the other person always waited for *you* to begin, you see nobody would ever say anything, so that –', but it is not where this book leaves us – the transparent vellum pages mean that we can always see a way out, as through a window, and we always have the option to move on, as in the closing words of the collection 'I turn the page'.

*

Writing an essay on whether there had been a Scottish literature, T.S. Eliot decided there was, briefly, but hadn't been for some centuries. It lacks the 'continuity of the language'; it is a provincial literature…. He was responding to a writer, one G. Gregory Smith, who had coined the phrase 'the Caledonian anti-syzygy' to describe the warring contraries that make up the Scottish tradition. To Smith, the absence of the settled identity Eliot finds in England is an opportunity, and makes Scotland the distinctive entity it is. To Eliot, it just means incoherent provincialism. Writing his great poems in Scots, Hugh MacDiarmid draws heavily on Jamieson's *Etymological Dictionary of the Scottish Language*. When composing the lovely 'Water Music', MacDiarmid has access to the first of its two volumes but not the second; hence the preponderance in that poem of Scots words beginning with letters from the first half of the dictionary.

(David Wheatley)

*

A message from the poet Harry Gilonis headed 'Pardon my French' with the following image attached:

And a question: how would I translate 'loin du ciel', literally or idiomatically? I'm not sure what he means by literally or idiomatically here, I can only see one way of translating this, 'far from the sky', and I'm not sure what I'm looking at. Is it a wine box, or a poem, an Ian Hamilton Finlay, or one of his followers? 'L'OISEAU LOIN DU CIEL' ('Bird far from the sky') seems to work together, like a minimalist poem, but what are the numbers doing here? Without thinking too much I send back the following potential translations (the fourth and fifth with an eye on Harry's 'idiomatically'):

> Bird far from the sky?
> Bird far from sky?
> A bird far from the sky?
> The bird far from home?
> Duck out of water?

Harry writes back explaining that the photo is of an embroidered cushion by Ian Hamilton Finlay, and that the letters identify ports on the northern coast of France, Caen and Saint-Malo, the letters-plus-numbers making up the official registration codes of two fishing-boats. *L'Oiseau*, he says, was a demersal, or groundfish, trawler; *Loin du ciel* he hasn't been able to trace. He adds a note saying that Finlay liked the found poetry he could get from such sources with Scottish boats from Peterhead, linking PD294 *Odysseus* with PD301 *Traveller*, and PD109 *Fruitful Bough* with PD110 *Honey Bee*, and that he must have been doing something similar with the French boats. Given Finlay's grasp of French, however, he adds, he can't begin to reconstruct it. The less French you have, I reply, only half tongue-in-cheek, the richer it becomes:

> Bird / lion of the sky
> Bird / sky lion
> Leisure / loin seal

*

Ludwig Wittgenstein on the poems of Georg Trakl: 'I do not understand them, but their tone delights me. It is the tone of a man of real genius.'

*

Poetry is common speech (T.S. Eliot). Poetry 'makes strange', or defamiliarises, and by doing so makes us see again (Wordsworth, Shklovsky). Poetry is good craic (Seamus Deane). Or, like Tom Leonard's reimagining of the Ten Commandments in Scots, 'Feed Ma Lamz', it is all of these things at once, and then some:

> Amyir gaffirz Gaffir. Hark.
>
> > nay fornirz ur communists
> > nay langwij
> > nay lip
> > nay laffn ina sunday
> > nay g.b.h. (septina wawr)
> > nay nooky huntn
> > nay tea-leaven
> > nay chanty rasslin
> > nay nooky huntn nix doar
> > nur kuvitn their ox
>
> Oaky doaky. Stick way it
> – rahl burn thi lohta yiz.

*

I remember talking to Sean Bonney once about teaching creative writing. He took a long drag on his cigarette, exhaled, and said: 'Nothing beats Bernadette Mayer'. He was talking about Mayer's 'Experiments', and he was right. To this day they still have the power to inspire:

Note what happens for a few days, hours (any space of time that has a limit you set); then look for relationships, connections, synchronicities; make something of it (writing).

Get a group of words (make a list or select at random); then form these words (only) into a piece of writing – whatever the words allow. Let them demand their own form, and/or: Use certain words in a set way, like, the same word in every line, or in a certain place in every paragraph, etc. Design words.

Write exactly as you think, as close as you can come to this, that is, put pen to paper & don't stop.

Make a pattern of repetitions.

They remind me of the methods employed by CAConrad, Raymond Queneau, Lyn Hejinian and Holly Pester. But as I read them again now, I see too how they must have inspired Sean Bonney's own writings: 'Cut-ups, paste-ups. etc. (Intersperse different material in horizontal cut-up strips, paste it together, infinite variations on this).' (Was Bonney thinking of this when he did his text collages?); 'Rewrite someone else's writing. Maybe someone formidable.' (And was this what inspired his rewritings of Baudelaire, and Rimbaud?)

Bibliography

Andrews, Bruce, and Bernstein, Charles (eds), *The L=A=N=G=U=A=G=E Book* (Carbondale and Edwardsville: Southern Illinois University Press, 1984).

Ashbery, John, and Brainard, Joe, *The Vermont Notebook* (Los Angeles: Black Sparrow Press, 1975).

Campion, Thomas, *Observations on the Art of English Poesie* (London: Richard Field, 1602).

Cockburn, Ken, and Finlay, Alec (eds), *The Order of Things* (Edinburgh: Polygon, 2001).

Devlin, Joe, *A Taxonomy of Protruding Bookmarks* (Malmö: Timglaset, 2024).

Fitterman, Robert, *Poems for Buildings* (Durham: If a Leaf Falls Press, 2022).

Halsey, Alan, *Versions of Martial* (Manchester: Knives Forks and Spoons Press, 2021).

Leonard, Tom, *outside the narrative* (London: Etruscan/World Power, 2011).

Morgan, Edwin, *Themes on a Variation* (Manchester: Carcanet, 1988).

Nichol, B.P., *Translating Translating Apollinaire* (Milwaukee: Membrane Press, 1979).

Schmidt, Michael, *Lives of the Poets* (London: Weidenfeld & Nicholson, 1988).

Smith, Rachel, *breath:e st(utter)ance* (Malmö: Timglaset, 2023).

Terry, Philip, *Oulipoems 2* (Toronto: Ahadada, 2009).

Trakl, Georg, *Selected Poems*, transl. by Robert Grenier, Michael Hamburger, David Luke and Christopher Middleton (London: Jonathan Cape, 1968).

Wheatley, David, *Stretto* (London: CB Editions, 2022).

Three Poems

GAIL McCONNELL

Another Attempt at a Fish Poem

The snailfish hasn't got a spiral home.
A body writing body, white on black
down in the hadal zone; more ghost than fish

the deepest-dwelling creature caught by lens.
Sensing no light, a scrivener of self,
it moves in flounces pinkish-wispy-white.

A shelllless being, as the lllls imply
the snailfish has its length – translucently
it flows; all flesh, gelatinous and slow.

How do I enter the poem or the zone
of impossible pressure and darkness
where a silence somehow caverns like death

(with *your* death – when you left in October)
while the creature slips out of the triplet
mucking up grief by still living?

A Tender Document
i.m. Ciaran Carson

I tend not to
notice dates but can't
not know it's one
year to the day
you left –
        my love
is working in
the kitchen making
offers fixing
prices fingers moving
over the board

what future there
is I can't
picture going over
all your poems I see
you laid out in the parlour
not speaking
in the room for it
silent never still
your music going
turning going
on

When I go
to pay in English
shops I hate
the part that always
comes the keeper
looking at my
notes the same
phrase hovering
in the air it's legal
tender legal
tender I repeat

The name for it
she says you really
haven't come across
it weird I
write these all
the time it's just
a tender document
responding to whatever call
or invitation came
you cost up how to execute
the work the second
party makes the call & once

it's on the clock
is ticking

When we would meet
in Caffè Nero
down in town on
Lombard Street
our time was never
unaccompanied
notes exchanged
at first we're quiet eyes
on the barista tending always
to the time & weight
& pressure

whirring beans go through
the burr – the orange
wrung into expression
on our table
my Ponge your Ponge first – each
ground & tamped & passed through
giving up their form
for something
we'll remember or
we won't the crema pressed
out through two spouts

a submission in response
she says that's all a tender
is the dates the cost a record
of just how
it shall be done

I loved it when
our time stretched to a second
cup the second being always
a cortado I've mixed up
with what you'd sometimes
say about remember & record their roots
in *cord* the heart remembering
recording practising as birds in song

to know the tune by heart
& carry it cortado
though is something else
the root is cut –
to you
I tilt this cup

'To Autumn' Variation
a rearrangement of Keats

                                          (Think not of the patient, sallow, sitting at the river-edge;
                  spring songs budding in the head-store; cricket song across the hedge.)

A kernel in its shell
conspiring music

as light and time swell
and fill the hazel, apple, gourd.

                                                                         poppies fume
                                                                          where dying blooms

                                                                          gnats mourn
                                                                          the soft breast

                                                                          the cells
                                                                          o'er-brimm'd

                                       Still,

bees zing
lambs bleat

moss'd trees
bend the hours

are sweet
and swallows gather.

                       All lives
                       and dies.

                       The red
                       mists lift.

                       Clouds touch
                       bosom-soft.

                                                                  Cease now
                                                                  as all choir,
                                                                whistle and twitter.

                                                                  Rosy hours.
                                                                Last skies.

Borges, Recursion and the Multiverse

Some Reflections

RICHARD GWYN

In his essay 'When Fiction Lives in Fiction' (1939), Borges states that he can trace his first notion of the problem of infinity to a large biscuit tin that lent 'mystery and vertigo' to his childhood. 'On the side of this unusual object,' he writes, 'there was a Japanese scene; I cannot remember the children or warriors depicted there, but I do remember that in a corner of that image the same biscuit tin reappeared with the same picture, and within it the same picture again, and so on (at least, potentially) into infinity…'[1]

This childhood experience of Borges's, in turn, evokes the vertigo the reader might feel before the various mysteries and labyrinths, the doublings and redoublings, and the recursive modes of narration that populate so many of the author's stories. And it is this notion of recursion (or recurrent self-referentiality) that I wish to address and explore today.

Of course, I don't know what biscuit tin Borges had in mind, but I definitely remember this one, from my own childhood, which, like his, contains on the lid an image of itself, and within that image another, and so on ad infinitum. Like the young Borges, I remember being enthralled by the image.

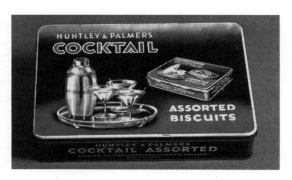

A dozen or so years ago I was invited by the Argentine newspaper *Clarín* to write a piece commemorating the twenty-fifth anniversary of Borges's death. At around the same time, as chance would have it, I wrote a piece for the British newspaper the *Independent* for their series 'Book of a Lifetime', in which writers were invited to contribute short summaries of a favourite book. I chose Borges's *Fictions*, and claimed that 'other books have had a powerful impact on me, but none marked a turning-point in my understanding of the world and the written word in quite the same way'. In both articles I began by describing the circumstances in which I was living when I first came across the work of the Argentine author, more or less as I record them here.

I discovered Borges's short stories at the age of eighteen, when I was living in an abandoned shepherd's hut at the foot of a mountain named Keratókambos, on the island of Crete. I found the place while exploring a deserted stretch of the south coast of the island, and moved in for the summer. I had a few books with me; I had just devoured *The Brothers Karamazov* and *The Magic Mountain* in rapid succession, and the brevity and intensity of Borges's writing came as a revelation. Borges himself had something to say about big novels, as he articulated in the Prologue to *Ficciones* (1944): 'The composition of vast books is a laborious and impoverishing extravagance. To go on for five hundred pages developing an idea whose perfect oral exposition is possible in a few minutes! A better course of procedure is to pretend that these books exist and then to offer a résumé, a commentary.'[2] The idea that instead of writing voluminous books we can simply pretend that they exist had a profound appeal to the budding writer in me, horrified at the interminable exposition of those mighty tomes by Dostoyevsky and Mann. Borges's ludic style and brevity were much more attractive, and there was something enormously liberating, a kind of weightlessness, to the idea that by minimising the word count we might invoke extraordinary worlds without having to set them down with wearisome description, endless exposition and fatuous dialogue. If only things were so simple. The brevity of a literary work does not diminish its complexity, and the worlds one encounters in Borges's compact stories contain multitudes.

Fiction within Fiction

But more than anything else, all those years ago, I was seduced by the idea that every instant contains the potential for an infinity of outcomes – a recurring motif in Borges's work – or that our universe is only one in a multiplicity of possible universes; or, less appealingly, that rather than being the proprietors of our own consciousness, we are being dreamed by some other entity. These are not comfortable ideas to live with, pushing, as they do, at the edges of comprehension. Always dissatisfied with received wisdoms, these ideas took a hold on me early in life, and I have never abandoned them, nor felt inclined to do so.

Borges concludes his essay on 'When Fiction Lives in Fiction' with a summary of Flann O'Brien's novel *At Swim-Two-Birds* (which, it might be noted, he reviewed in the magazine *El Hogar* only six months after it first appeared in English), in which a young student from

---

1 In Borges, J.L., *The Total Library: Non-Fiction 1922–1986*, transl. Esther Allen (Penguin, 2001).
2 Borges, J.L., 'Prologue' to *Fictions*, transl. Anthony Kerrigan (Calder, 1991).

Dublin writes a novel about a publican from that city, who in turn writes a novel about his customers, one of whom is the student author; and he quotes Schopenhauer's comment, 'that dreaming and wakefulness are the pages of a single book, and that to read them in order is to live, and to leaf through them at random, to dream. Paintings within paintings and books that branch off into other books help us sense this oneness.' In other words, the perspective that one story was a vehicle for other stories, and that the process could become one of unlimited recursion, was established quite early in the writer's career, and over time it became a hallmark of his literary oeuvre.

A fundamental principle within the study of linguistics is that, in spoken language, an idea can be contained within an idea, a phrase within a phrase. This forms the basis of recursion in grammar. Noam Chomsky has claimed that it is the essential tool that underlies all of the creativity of human language. In theory, according to Chomsky, an infinitely long, recursive sentence is possible, since there is no limit to the mind's capacity to embed one thought within another. Our language is recursive because our minds are recursive.

A parody of the opening sentence of a now-forgotten novel, *Paul Clifford*, by the nineteenth-century English novelist Edward Bulwer-Lytton, might serve as an initial illustration of recursion – 'It was a dark and stormy night, and we said to the captain: "Tell us a story!" And this is the story the captain told: "It was a dark and stormy night, and we said to the captain, 'Tell us a story!' And this is the story the captain told: 'It was a dark and stormy night '"'...

Another exercise in recursion would be the English nursery rhyme about an old lady who swallows a fly, which, as the song's chorus repeats, 'wriggled and jiggled and tickled inside her'. The unfortunate woman decides to swallow a spider in order to catch the fly, and then successively, a bird to catch the spider, a cat to catch the bird, a dog to catch the cat, and so on in a theoretically infinite number of permutations. This gruesome little song neatly exemplifies the nature of recursion and, as I discovered, is even used as an illustration in a computer science programming manual on that topic. An article on recursive thinking in *American Scientist* points out that the realisation that one has thoughts about one's own thoughts itself constitutes a theory of mind.[3] René Descartes is renowned for the phrase *cogito, ergo sum* (although he actually wrote 'je pense, donc je suis': I think, therefore I am). Descartes presented this utterance as proof of his own existence, and although he sometimes doubted it, the doubt was itself a mode of thinking, so his real existence was not in doubt. The phrase is fundamentally recursive, since it involves not only thinking, but thinking about thinking.

Remembering a particular episode from one's own life suggests a recursive projection of oneself out of the present moment. In the novel *À la recherche du temps perdu*, Marcel Proust returns to various projections of episodic memory, including the famous moment when the taste of a petite madeleine evokes the memory of a past event in the narrator's mind. In terms of the present text, we might consider as recursive the references I made a few moments ago, when I said that I started an article in *Clarín* twelve years ago with (almost) the same words that I used today, or when I recited the words: 'All those years ago, I was seduced by the idea that every instant contains the potential for an infinity of outcomes.'

The notion of recursion is also the driving force behind fractals, complex patterns that are self-replicating across different scales. Fractals are created by repeating a simple process over and over in an ongoing feedback loop. It has been claimed that the coast of Brittany has the characteristics of a fractal, for example, and we are all familiar with those windmilling patterns used to illustrate fractals, with images reminiscent of the hippy era and psychedelic drugs.

Once I begin to seek out instances of recursion in the works of Borges, Google leads me down a rabbit hole of articles on Borges and the infinite, Borges and Buddhism, Borges and quantum mechanics, Borges and the multiverse, as well, of course, as better-known works on the writer, such as Guillermo Martínez's study *Borges and Mathematics*. It is as if, for my sins, I have stepped inside the Library of Babel, given that the internet is the ultimate manifestation of that accursed and infinite library, and itself an unparalleled example of recursion. The Library of Babel has also been represented as a fractal, or a series of fractals, in the work of various artists, and the creators of one website – the *babel image archives* – uses images instead of letters of the alphabet to reproduce, as its creators claim, every image that ever has been or could be created within its chosen colour palette.

Recursive Objects

In Martínez's book there is much to give us pause for thought. Of particular note, in the first of his essays, is a reference to what he calls *recursive objects*: 'It is possible to isolate this curious property of infinity and apply it to other objects or other situations in which a part of the object contains key information to the whole. We'll call them recursive objects.' For example, he reminds us that 'from a biological point of view, a human being is a recursive object. A single human cell is enough to generate a clone [...] Certain mosaics are clearly recursive objects: in particular, those in which the design inherent in the first few tiles is repeated throughout.' Martínez is a mathematician, as well as a novelist, and there is, among his various explanations – which we do not have time to go into now – an account of mathematical infinity in which it is shown that the whole is not necessarily greater than each of the parts: 'There are certain parts that are as great as the whole. There are parts that are equivalent to the whole.'[4]

---

3 Corballis, Michael C., 'The Uniqueness of Human Recursive Thinking' in *American Scientist*, Vol 95 No. 3, 2007.
4 Martínez, G., *Borges and Mathematics*, transl. Andrea G. Labinger (Purdue University Press, 2012).

In the works of Borges, the supreme recursive objects are libraries and labyrinths. I have made reference to the Library of Babel – itself a labyrinth – and we know from various sources that the labyrinth was a foundational myth for young Georgie, as he was known by his family. In 1971 Borges was interviewed by the Economics Nobel laureate and renowned computer scientist Herbert Simon, one of the founding investigators of Artificial Intelligence, who was visiting Buenos Aires. This improbable meeting of minds was set up at Simon's request. The conversation took place in English. In attendance, but not participating, was the writer Gabriel Zadunaisky, who recorded and translated the interview for the weekly journal *Primera Plana*.[5] At the start of the interview, Simon asks Borges about the origins of his fascination with labyrinths, to which Borges replies that he could remember having seen an engraving of a labyrinth 'in a French book'. Borges tells Simon that he used to gaze at this engraving of the labyrinth, and adds, a little ironically, that if he had had a magnifying glass, he might have been able to make out the shape of the Minotaur within its corridors. Simon, playing along, asks him if he ever found it, to which Borges replies, 'As a matter of fact my eyesight was never very good'. And then, a little incongruously: 'Later I discovered a little about life's complexity, as if it were a game. I'm not talking about chess now.' At least, this appears to be what he says. In the text published by *Primera Plana*, the words are 'No me refiero al ajedrez en este caso' (I'm not referring to chess here) but, bizarrely, in the Rodríguez Monegal biography (written in English) they become the exact opposite: 'I'm talking about chess now'. There follows a passage in the interview in which Borges remarks on the play of words (in English) by which 'maze' is included within the word 'amazement', and he comments to Simon: 'That's the way that I regard life. A continuous amazement. A continuous bifurcation of the labyrinth.'[6] I would ask you to hang on to this remark. We will return to it shortly.

Guillermo Martínez also reminds us that in Borges's short parable 'On Exactitude in Science', there is another example of recursion, when the map of a single province occupies the space it was originally designed to represent, and with the years it falls apart, until its tattered ruins 'are inhabited by animals and beggars'.[7] Furthermore, Borges refers several times in his works to the map of Josiah Royce, a map which is perfectly traced on a small tract of English soil, and which is so precise that it contains within it a map of itself, which in turn contains a map of the map, and so on.

We might add to these examples the recursivity of *A Thousand and One Nights* that Borges references in both 'The Garden of Forking Paths' as well as in 'When Fiction Lives in Fiction'. In this second text, as Borges reminds us, the murderous king appears to himself in one of the stories he is being told. To quote from the essay:

> None of them is as disturbing as that of night 602, a piece of magic among the nights. On that strange night, the king hears his own story from the queen's lips. He hears the beginning of the story, which includes all the others, and also – monstrously – itself. Does the reader have a clear sense of the vast possibility held out by this interpolation, its peculiar danger? Were the queen to persist, the immobile king would forever listen to the truncated story of the thousand and one nights, now infinite and circular [...] In *The Thousand and One Nights*, Scheherazade tells many stories; one of them is, almost, the story of *The Thousand and One Nights*.[8]

Incidentally, Julio Cortázar's short story 'The Continuity of Parks' addresses the same notion, which is certainly no coincidence.

Tlön, Uqbar, Orbis Tertius

And so it is that I return to the origin, to the source of my enduring Borgesian adventure, re-reading the first of his stories that I encountered, 'Tlön, Uqbar, Orbis Tertius', in which Borges describes a fictional country, Uqbar, whose mythology originates from a mysterious world called Tlön. The story was first published in issue 68 of the magazine *Sur*, in May 1940, and contains a postscript, dated 1947, in which the reader learns that objects made in Uqbar have begun to make their way here, to 'our' world. The postscript also informs the reader that the author has reproduced the preceding article just as it appeared on its first publication in 1940, 'omitting no more than some figures of speech, and a kind of burlesque summing up, which now strikes me as frivolous. So many things have happened since that date [...] I will confine myself to putting them down.'[9] A curious opening, perhaps, to an impossible postscript, but what strikes the reader attentive to the notion of recursion is that, as Rodríguez Monegal has pointed out, 'in the same way that the label of a tin of biscuits shows a picture of a tin of biscuits and so on, creating an infinite regression, Borges' text was originally published in the sixty-eighth issue of *Sur* as a reproduction of a text already published in the sixty-eighth edition of *Sur*'.[10]

'Tlön, Uqbar, Orbis Tertius' marked a turning point in Borges's evolution as a writer. First of all, the story stands as a melding together of the essayistic and the fictional, in a way that would become a staple of the

---

5 *Primera Plana*, 'Borges–Simon, detrás del laberinto. Herbert Simon y Jorge Luis Borges' IX, 414 (5 January 1971).
6 Monegal, Emir Rodríguez, *Jorge Luis Borges: A Literary Biography* (Paragon House: 1988).
7 Borges, J.L., 'On Exactitude in Science', *Collected Fictions*, transl. Andrew Hurley (Penguin, 1998).
8 'When Fiction Lives in Fiction' (ibid).
9 'Tlön, Uqbar, Orbis Tertius', transl. Alastair Reid, in *Fictions* (ibid).
10 Monegal, Emir Rodríguez (ibid).

writer's work henceforth. And while the story's form blurs the distinction between genres, the content veers towards fantastical or speculative fiction. And, significantly, there is a giveaway line near the start of the story that suggests its recursive and self-referential status: the story itself evolves out of a discussion Borges is having with Adolfo Bioy Casares about 'a novel in the first person, whose narrator would omit or disfigure the facts and indulge in various contradictions which would permit a few readers – very few readers – to perceive an atrocious or banal reality'. We, the readers, might therefore deduce that this hypothetical novel is in fact the very story we are reading, and that the imaginary world is actually Earth – 'Orbis Tertius', as it was referred to in Renaissance cosmography.

As those who know the story will recall, Uqbar is a fictional place, originally conceived as a territory somewhere in Asia Minor, although this idea is quickly dropped. Tlön is presented first as a 'region', and then as a planet, which serves to provide the people of Uqbar with a mythology. All of the literature of Uqbar derives from or is set in Tlön. However, as we come to learn, the planet Tlön does not exist: it is a fiction within a fiction, a hoax that has been invented by a secret society founded by a millionaire, Ezra Buckley, in the nineteenth century. As a part of the hoax, stories about Tlön, and even some of its artefacts, have gradually been released into our world in an attempt to convince people of its reality. Putting it simply – and in terms that Borges himself might have avoided – Tlön is the unconscious of the fictitious country, Uqbar, its realm of myth and dream.

At one memorable point in the story, Borges describes one of the oldest regions of Tlön, in which it is a not uncommon occurrence for lost objects to be duplicated: 'Two people are looking for a pencil; the first one finds it and says nothing; the second finds a second pencil, no less real, but more in keeping with his expectation. These secondary objects are called *hrönir* and, even though awkward in form, are a little larger than the originals. Until recently the *hrönir* were the accidental children of absentmindedness and forgetfulness.'

The search for the pencil results in two discoveries: in one of these, the pencil is the 'authentic' one that the protagonist lost, and in the other the pencil is a simulacrum (or *hrön*), a possible version of itself. This process of replication is repeated several times over, as Borges explains:

> [T]he *hrönir* of the second and third degree – that is, the *hrönir* derived from another *hrön*, and the *hrönir* derived from the *hrön* of a *hrön* – exaggerate the flaws of the original; those of the fifth degree are almost uniform; those of the ninth can be confused with those of the second; and those of the eleventh degree have a purity of form which the originals do not possess. The process is a recurrent one; a *hrön* of the twelfth degree begins to deteriorate in quality. Stranger and more perfect than any *hrön* is sometimes the *ur*, which is a thing produced by suggestion, an object brought into being by hope. The great gold mask I mentioned previously is a distinguished example.[11]

It seems likely that Borges took the word *hrön* from the almost identical Icelandic *hrönn* (plural *hrannir*), meaning 'wave'. Alongside the connotations of continuous movement, re-shaping and re-formulation associated with waves in the sea, we might note that the term 'wave function', as defined by Schrödinger in 1928, has a distinct meaning in quantum mechanics, namely that 'a wave function is defined as a function describing the probability of a particle's quantum state as a function of position, momentum, time, and/or spin.'[12] I do not know whether Borges was familiar with wave function theory in 1940. If he was, then he was making a private joke detectable to only a few – very few – readers, but if he did not, his selection of the word 'hrön' to define something in a state of almost constant change was remarkably prescient.

While Borges is clearly having a lot of fun with the erratic behaviour of his *hrönir*, there is also something disturbing about this incessant duplication of things, especially in the detail about those pencils, which reappear in a slightly different form from the versions that were lost. Are we to believe that all replication involves a divergence from the original? There is a vagueness, or a spectrality, even, that reminds one (since bits of Borges always remind one of other bits of Borges) of the indeterminacy possessed by various other objects in his work, from stones to tigers.

This, in part, is the subject of an unpublished essay by Kevin Wilson, titled 'Of Stones and Tigers: Time, Infinity, Recursion and Liminality in the writings of JL Borges'. In this enterprising study, the author points to the enclosure in 'The Circular Ruins' that is described as being 'crowned by the stone figure of a horse or tiger'; and the way, in 'The Immortal', that the city of the immortals appears to the protagonist as resembling 'the body of a tiger or a bull pullulating with teeth, organs and heads monstrously yoked together yet hating each other'; or the way, in 'Dreamtigers', Borges tells us that his dreams have begun to yield, instead of a recognisable tiger, an approximate being, 'looking more like a dog or a bird'. Isn't it strange, in such a writer, otherwise so unequivocal, so exacting, so focused on clarity, that a tiger – the creature most hallowed in Borges's personal mythology – should somehow be confounded with a horse, a bull, a dog or a bird? Unless, of course, that confusion is intentional, that it is a part of the point. But what is the point? That whatever is dreamed or willed is subject to external manipulation by forces unseen? That everything is an approximation of something else? That the pencil you hold in your hand might

---

11 'Tlön, Uqbar, Orbis Tertius' (ibid).
12 Helmenstine, Anne Marie, 'What is a Wave Function?' ThoughtCo, Jun. 25, 2024, thoughtco.com/definition-of-wavefunction-605790.

be simply the replica of another pencil lost in a contiguous world? That everything is an element in the infinite process of recursion?

Shortly after writing the above passage, I was due to teach a group of graduate students in the university where I work, and had intended to use 'Tlön, Uqbar, Orbis Tertius' as the text for that week's seminar. The night before the class I dreamed that the story in my copy of the book differed in small but significant ways from the original, that it was in fact a *hrön* of the original story. In reality, I had bought my copy of the book, *Fictions,* many years before in a cheap edition, the cover of which displayed a badly drawn image of something midway between the Eye of Providence and a vagina. My copy of the story was a fake. I awoke in a state of anxiety, worried that I would not be able to retrieve the true story in time for my class. It was only later that I realised, of course, that my version was an English translation of Borges's story, by Alastair Reid, and that all translations are, after a fashion, *hrönir*.

Borges ends the main part of his story, before embarking on his fallacious postscript, with an elegant passage summarising the process of recursion in Tlön:

> Things duplicate themselves in Tlön. They tend at the same time to efface themselves, to lose their detail when people forget them. The classic example is that of a stone threshold which lasted as long as it was visited by a beggar, and which faded from sight on his death. Occasionally, a few birds, a horse perhaps, have saved the ruins of an amphitheatre.[13]

If I might be permitted a further biographical intrusion: the phrase 'un umbral que perduró mientras lo visitaba un mendigo' (a threshold which lasted as long as it was visited by a beggar) evokes the stone hut in which I was living when I read the story (in the original it is simply an 'umbral' – threshold – whereas in the English translation by Alastair Reid, it is rendered as 'stone threshold', reminding us, obliquely, of Borges's famous collocation, in 'Borges and I', of 'stones and tigers'). At one point during that summer of 1975, I had to travel to the island's capital, Iraklion, to pick up mail. On returning to the cabin I found, to my surprise, that someone had paid a visit during my absence. Lying beside the open entrance to the hut was a bottle of the local home distilled spirit, *tsikoudia*, and a small box of *loukoumi* (Turkish delight) wrapped in a coarse ribbon. I was confused as to who might have left such a gift. The mystery was resolved a few days later when a lithe, elderly Cretan appeared as I sat reading – as was my habit – at the hut's threshold. He was, he told me, the owner of the place, but he had no use for it any more. He had noticed some time ago that I had moved in, and was curious to meet me. I could, he said, stay for as long as I wished. I brewed coffee and conversed with him in my pidgin Greek, illustrated with much gesticulation and mime. He was a perfect gentleman, this elderly Cretan from the days before tourism laid waste to the country: enigmatic, generous, gifted with a subtle sense of humour, he accepted my occupancy of the hut as an act of providence. He seemed pleased that I was there. In a sense, I was carrying out the function of the beggar in Borges's story: for my host, perhaps, the hut only had purpose (or reality) for as long as someone lived in it.

Countless Worlds

As I have suggested, one of the things that first attracted me to Borges was his willingness to address the theme of the infinite permutations of chance. It is well known how often Borges referred to chance, whether in his stories, in his essays, or his poems. And long before I'd ever heard of parallel universes or the many worlds hypothesis, I was pretty much obsessed by the notion that every decision I took led to an outcome, or rather, a series of outcomes, which, had I chosen differently, would have led to different life circumstances, not just for me, but for others around me.

To use a footballing analogy, it used to bother me when a sports commentator would say 'if he hadn't missed that goal in the first half, the score would now be 2–1'. No! If he hadn't missed that goal something else would have happened, and then something else; every moment of the game would have unfolded in a totally different way from the way it did by the missing or the scoring of the goal. Just as in life, to cite a few examples, what would have happened if I hadn't stepped into the road in front of that car in Leytonstone in 1976; or, that night in July, 1984, if I hadn't stayed on at the Café d'Artagnan for one more drink; or, if I had taken the bus rather than the metro on a particular night in Athens in 1986, the course of my life would no doubt have been different. True, the outcomes would often have been trivial, but they might, on the other hand, have been life-changing.

The term 'sliding-door moment' has become shorthand for this line of thinking, following the film of that name, starring Gwyneth Paltrow, but the concept itself is much older – and is, as we know, a staple in the fictions of Borges.

Hugh Everett, a Princeton PhD student, published a thesis in 1957 in which he claimed that we are living in a multiverse in which exist countless copies of each world's contents, including ourselves. As Everett's biographer, Peter Byrne, explains: 'the wave function of an observer would, in effect, bifurcate at each interaction of the observer with a superposed object'. Thus every choice or decision in the course of a life precipitates the splitting of the universe, which then continues to split, infinitely, with each decisive turn that follows. As Byrne puts it: 'Each branch has its own copy of the observer, a copy that perceived one of those alternatives as the outcome [...] each branch embarks on a different future, independently of the others.'[14]

---

13 'Tlön, Uqbar, Orbis Tertius' (ibid).
14 Peter Byrne, 'The Many Worlds of Hugh Everett', *Scientific American* (December 2007).

At the time, Everett's theory was rejected by the then reigning authority in quantum mechanics, Niels Bohr, and Everett, disgusted by academia, gave up theoretical physics and went to work for the Pentagon as a probability analyst, in which his work included the prediction of various scenarios of nuclear Armageddon. However, among a small group of followers, his hypothesis lived on, grew in momentum, and is now regarded by many of today's leading quantum theorists as foundational. According to one of the most eminent of those physicists, Max Tegmark of the Massachusetts Institute of Technology, Everett's discovery is 'as important as Einstein's work on relativity'.[15]

The idea that our world is one of many parallel worlds that branch off from each other, moment by moment, without intersecting or communicating, with the result that each permutation of every event has the potential to occur somewhere, is both appealing and terrifying. On a personal level, there is some comfort, to me at least, in imagining that all the bad decisions I ever took have – in some distant world – been counteracted by better ones. On the other hand, there is the moral dilemma of knowing that by making certain choices in this world, one runs the risk, almost by definition, of setting off a chain of events that will have negative ramifications elsewhere in the multiverse. After some consideration, however, one might come to the conclusion that the best way to live in a multiverse of many worlds is to be mindful of the way you live your life in this one.

The passage in Borges that has drawn comparisons with Everett's hypothesis occurs in 'The Garden of Forking Paths'. In this story, which takes place in England during the First World War, the protagonist, Yu Tsun, is working for the Germans as a spy. Yu Tsun, who is Chinese (and who despises Germany as a 'barbarous country') is being pursued by a British agent named Richard Madden, who is in fact Irish, a detail – reflecting those that besiege Yu Tsun himself – that already suggests divided loyalties. Yu Tsun has information of great importance to the German war effort, but with Madden closing in on him, is unable to pass this on to his masters in Berlin (nor do we, the readers, learn what this information consists of until the final paragraph). He goes, inexplicably, as it seems at first, to the house of Dr Stephen Albert, a renowned Sinologist with a special research interest in Ts'ui Pên, Tsun's grandfather, a respected sage, who retired as Governor of Yunnan Province in order to write a vast novel and to create a maze 'in which all men would lose themselves'. He spent thirteen years absorbed in these tasks before he was assassinated by a stranger. His novel had no sense to it and nobody ever found his labyrinth. It turns out, this being Borges, that the book and the labyrinth were one and the same thing, and the title of this infinite and chaotic novel is, of course, 'The Garden of Forking Paths'.

Albert tells Yu Tsun that Ts'ui Pên's novel is modelled on a labyrinth in the sense that it constantly bifurcates in time, but not in space. 'In all fiction,' he explains, 'when a man is faced with alternatives he chooses one at the expense of the others.' However, in this novel, whenever a course of action has to be decided upon, rather than choosing one and pursuing its linear development, each course taken divides in two, with each of these being the point of departure for other, further, bifurcations, and so on. As Dr Albert explains:

> Your ancestor [...] believed in an infinite series of times, in a dizzily growing, ever-spreading network of diverging, converging and parallel times. This web of time – the strands of which approach one another, bifurcate, intersect, or ignore each other through the centuries – embraces every possibility. We do not exist in most of them. In some you exist and not I, while in others I do, and you do not, and in yet others both of us exist. In this one, in which chance has favoured me, you have come to my gate. In another, you, crossing the garden, have found me dead. In yet another, I say these very same words, but am an error, a phantom.
>
> 'In all of them,' I enunciated, with a tremor in my voice, 'I deeply appreciate and am grateful for the restoration of Ts'ui Pên's garden.'
>
> 'Not in *all*,' he murmured with a smile. 'Time is forever dividing itself towards innumerable futures and in one of them you are my enemy.'
>
> Once again I sensed the pullulation of which I have already spoken. It seemed to me that the dew-damp garden surrounding the house was infinitely saturated with invisible people. All were Albert and myself, secretive, busy and multiform in other dimensions of time. I lifted my eyes and the short nightmare disappeared.[16]

After this brief elaboration on the nature of the multiverse, it almost comes as an anti-climax to learn that the only reason Yu Tsun has decided to come to this house is to murder Albert, whose name will be plastered all over the newspapers the following day, thereby informing Yu Tsun's spy chief in Berlin that Albert is the name of the French town from which the Allies are preparing a massive artillery offensive against the German lines. As others have remarked, the 'pullulation of possibilities' that Yu Tsun senses anticipates the many worlds hypothesis of the quantum physicist Hugh Everett by fifteen years. The similarities between Everett's hypothesis and Borges's story are encapsulated in corresponding passages from each work. In the fifth section of Everett's original article, we find:

> The 'trajectory' of the memory configuration of an observer performing a sequence of measurements is [...] not a linear sequence of memory configura-

---

15 Cited in the BBC documentary *Parallel Worlds, Parallel Lives*, dir. Louise Lockwood (2007).
16 'The Garden of Forking Paths' transl. Helen Temple and Ruthven Todd, in *Fictions* (1991).

tions, but a branching tree, with all possible outcomes existing simultaneously.[17]

And in Borges's story:

> In all fiction, when a man is faced with alternatives he chooses one at the expense of the others. In the almost unfathomable Ts'ui Pên, he chooses – simultaneously – all of them. He thus *creates* various futures, various times that start others that will in their turn branch out and bifurcate in other times.

Daniel Balderstone, in his book *How Borges Wrote,* states that Borges's tendency 'to write with numerous variations and possibilities in mind, adding layers by accretion, then re-writing several more times […] means that his creative process involved the weaving together of textual fragments into provisional, not definitive wholes. It is almost,' he continues, 'as though Borges were enacting his own version of the many worlds theory in his writing practice.' Elsewhere, Balderstone comments that '[t]hese reflections on myriad possibilities, in manuscripts that are themselves vast semantic fields of possibilities, show that Borges worked out on the page the formal features of his linguistic games with some precision, leaving hints of this process in the final texts. What historians of science have noticed as an early version of the "many worlds hypothesis" is of a piece with Borges' poetics of prose, itself a literary corollary of the uncertainty principle.' But if this is the case, I would venture, Borges is by no means alone in such practices.

And before we become too overawed by Borges's apparent act of precognition, it should be noted, following Dominic Moran, in an essay titled 'Borges and the Multiverse' (2012), that there is clear evidence that Borges borrowed (or plagiarised) key features of his story from the English science fiction writer Olaf Stapledon (1886–1950) – most notably from his novel *Star Maker* (1937) – as well as from a famous Chinese novel translated into English as *The Dream of the Red Chamber,* both of which Borges had reviewed in the Argentine magazine *El Hogar* in November 1937. Not only this, but, as Moran eloquently asserts:

> Regarding the question of Borges' (or rather Stapledon's) clairvoyance, it might be remarked that if Everett's theory or some refinement of it turns out to be true, then it was inevitable that not just in one but in countless universes 'Borges', or some version of him, should have written a story prior to the emergence of the theory, just as it was inevitable that in countless others still 'he' or one of his avatars […] should have written innumerable versions which differ by a comma, a full stop, a letter, a word etc (I could go on – endlessly) from the one that we

have. In other words – and this is one of the bizarre but strictly logical consequences of a multiverse in which anything can happen – he deserves absolutely no credit for it.[18]

Parallel Worlds, Parallel Lives

Whether or not Borges knew of the theories of quantum mechanics is addressed quite specifically in a short article by the physicist Alberto G. Rojo, who fell into conversation with the author on 9 July 1985, and asked him whether he knew that his work was referenced in the work of several notable physicists. Borges's answer is revealing: 'How strange! This is really curious because the only thing I know about physics comes from my father, who once showed me how a barometer works.' 'He said it,' Rojo, tells us, 'with an oriental modesty, moving his hands as though trying to draw the apparatus in the air. And then he added: "Physicists are so imaginative!"'[19]

In Rojo's opinion, the similarity between the two texts just cited indicates 'the extraordinary way Borges's mind was immersed in the cultural matrix of the twentieth century, in that complex web whose secret components ramify beyond the demarcations between disciplines […] While Everett's […] ideas can be read as science fiction, in 'The Garden of Forking Paths', fiction can be read as science.'

In the documentary film *Parallel Worlds, Parallel Lives*, Hugh Everett's son, Mark, who happens to be lead singer for the rock band The Eels, travels across the United States in search of the father he barely knew. The story is both informative and moving. As has been noted, Hugh Everett's theories were rejected in his lifetime, and he ended up a rather miserable and lonely man, consumed by a sense of loss and sinking into alcoholism, a state no doubt exacerbated by the apocalyptic tedium of the work he carried as an analyst for the Pentagon. There is something essentially Borgesian about the son's quest for his father – the man who devised the single most astonishing theory of quantum mechanics – and his recognition of similarities between the two of them; and in an especially poignant section of the film, he reveals, in the cellar of his home, boxes and boxes filled with his father's notebooks. Watching the documentary, it is as if Ts'ui Pên's labyrinth has at last been tracked down in the basement of this mildly eccentric and self-effacing musician.

Earlier I referred to the Proustian notion that remembering a particular episode from one's own life is nothing less than a recursive projection of oneself out of the present. And so it is that the association of my first encounter with the stories of Borges amid the landscape of Crete, with its rugged mountains and its wine-dark sea, is indissoluble.

Reading outside my stone cabin at sunset, I heard an exchange of voices. In the distance, some way above me,

---

17 Everett, Hugh III, 'Relative State Formulation of Quantum Mechanics', *Reviews of Modern Physics*, Vol 29, No 3, 1957.
18 Moran, Dominic, 'Borges and the Multiverse: Some Further Thoughts', in *Bulletin of Spanish Studies,* Vol 89, No 6, 2012.
19 Rojo, Alberto J., 'The Garden of the Forking Worlds: Borges and Quantum Mechanics' Oakland Journal 9 (2005).

a man and a woman were calling to each other, each voice lifting with a strange buoyancy across the gorge that lay between one flank of the mountain and the next. Only the nearer figure, the man, was visible, and his voice seemed to rebound off the wall of the chasm, half a mile away. The woman remained out of sight, but her voice likewise drifted across the gorge, with an ethereal vibrancy. There were perhaps a dozen turns, and then silence. I listened, spellbound. And that brief exchange, that shouted conversation, with its unearthly sounds, the tension between the voices, the exhalations and long vowels echoing off the sides of the mountain, would haunt me for years, haunts me still.

They seemed to me to be speaking across time, that man and woman. Their ancestors, or other versions of themselves, had been having that conversation, exchanging those same sounds, that same music, across countless centuries. It was, for me, a lesson in both the durability and at the same time the fragility of our lives; that conversation, that calling across the chasm, represented a glimpse of eternity. And with this I am reminded that in 'The History of Eternity' Borges wrote of the idea of the infinite that it 'liberates us, even if for only a few moments, from the unbearable oppression of the passage of time'. In the interview with Herbert Simon, Borges utters the phrase I asked you to bear in mind: 'That's the way I regard life. A continuous amazement. A continuous bifurcation of the labyrinth.' Which in some way leads us back, in recursive fashion, to where we started, with Borges claiming that he could trace his first notion of the problem of infinity to that far distant biscuit tin.

But the moment passed, and continues to pass, lives on in my memory and imagination, and in so many memories that are the projections of myself out of the present, reminding us that of all the possible lives that each of us might live, we have this one, linked by an invisible thread to the innumerable lives that are unlived by us, but which – who knows – are even now being lived out by another version of ourselves in some other garden of forking paths. And having returned once more to that other, earlier life, I have ensured that this paper becomes an exercise in recursion in which I, the narrator, remember a previous self who wrote an article that recalls a stone cabin beneath a mountain where an even earlier version of that narrator discovers, for the first time, the stories of Jorge Luis Borges.

PNR

Poetry   News   Conversation   Reviews

SUBSCRIBE

Six issues of *PN Review* each year
Unlimited access to four decades of archive
Submit work for editorial consideration
Invitations to *PN Review* sponsored events
Discounts on promotions

WWW.PNREVIEW.CO.UK

'The most engaged, challenging and serious-minded of all the UK's poetry magazines.'
– Simon Armitage

Reviews

All Is Not Lost

Linda Black, *Interior* (Shearsman) £12.95

Jon Thompson, *The Distances* (Shearsman) £10.95

Reviewed by Ian Seed

Linda Black's *Interior* investigates what it means to be a person. The poems interrogate the ways in which we manufacture an identity for ourselves through our interpretation of events, relationships and memories, not least through the creation of art. They navigate the age-old question – who exactly is the 'I' that is doing the interpreting? Poignantly, they explore how our view of ourselves changes, fragments and grows unruly as we become older. One thread in these poems is the fear of losing memory altogether: however unreliable memory can be, it is all we have to maintain our sense of an 'I'. Yet at some point in our lives, how can we avoid having our 'head / blown' like 'dandelions' ('Something needs divining')?

The opening poem, 'Here I embark on the difficult task of creating a person', sets the Cartesian tone for the rest of the book:

> I have begun to examine 'her' mental state, her limited sense of reality, having existed thus far in her own head. Such inward focus blights her eyesight, condenses memory, maims concentration. *How to become (more) real?* Take her out of herself. No wonder she forgets the plot, the places she hasn't been.

All is not lost. The possibility of understanding and creating a life, both while living it and looking back, comes from making art (another process which Black examines and takes to task). For this, the artist must be open, 'without preparation', even if this may involve a 'scrabble for pieces I no longer recognise' ('I present myself'). As good a place as any to start is to make

> No promises
> no cake on the counter
> no reins to hold
> me backwards
>
> *to thine own self...* ('Come in')

Throughout this 114-page collection, there is a delight in word play and music in a kind of crafted spontaneity, reflecting something of Kerouac's bop prosody or what Clark Coolidge has called 'babble flow'. Fortunately, Linda Black's skills as a writer enable her to do so in a manner which heightens our sense of the reality of her bewilderments, losses and loves so that they become ours, too.

The Distances by Jon Thompson is linked to Black's collection in some of the ways in which philosophy is woven into its poetry, though its tone is very different. It employs long, enjambed lines and combines critical reflection with story-telling and elegy, at times reminiscent of Robinson Jeffers, and with echoes of Martin Heidegger in phrases such as 'the world that unworlded you' ('Fenestration at Dawn with Death') and 'the crystalline / thereness of being not-there' ('Ode to the Wind not in the Pindaric Mode'). Thompson scrutinizes how we try to capture being through language and symbolism, even though in a deeper sense this only takes us further away from an unnameable reality:

> O wind I need to apologise for
> centuries and centuries of mythologizing
>   it's just a sign of how ill-at-ease in the world we are
> it's easier see you as a symbol
>   than to accept your untranslatable freedom [...]
> if you had a mind what word would you use for
>   a world we weigh down with intention
> and many other kinds of heaviness
>   ('Ode to the Wind not in the Pindaric Mode')

Language is something that we have 'borrowed and have to give back' ('A Question of How Far Back You Want to Go'), for our time as members of the human race is finite. This may seem evident at an intellectual level, but Thompson through his potent, pantheistic use of imagery makes us wonder at finitude, language and human endeavour, and ultimately marvel at its beauty:

> It happens when the air is light and all at once
>   the cherry trees
>   lift the sky with white blossoms
> they're songs they have been singing this way
>   before there was song
>   every branch is a different poem and
> every year brings new poems in the air replacing
>   the old ones
> it all happens in daylight and is ordinary
>   as I walked under them the pavement
>   could not
> be seen for the bone-white blossoms blown
>   down
>   what to them is time it cannot be the same
>   as it is for us ('In Real Time').

As well as personal and philosophical reflection, *The Distances* draws on history and ancient myths from different parts of the world. Ultimately, whatever our losses, limitations and regrets – 'the impossibility of making it whole' ('Names Made for Us in Another Country') – Thompson shows we can do no other but wonder at the 'bigness of an impenitent blue sky / and the light / [...] unfettered' ('Cloud Time').

A Measureless Ouija-Board

Conflicted Copy, Sam Riviere (Faber) £10.99

Reviewed by Hal Coase

In poetry, as in love, it's the non-necessity of what follows that takes our breath away. Anything can happen. Anything can happen, and then whatever does happen could only have happened that way. We're well trained to pick over the second part of this happenstance. Most features of form can be thought of as allowing choices to seem *necessary*, before they come to seem either correct or beautiful, audacious or dull. Destiny, compulsion and fetish (like genre, metre and metaphor) are useful when we want to redescribe anything that happens as the only thing that could have happened. We often need them to talk ourselves down from the ledge of infinite possibility. The satisfaction that such redescriptions provide is in proportion to the dizziness and excitement that threatens to upturn them, and which they work to contain. In return, we get back a little kick of agency; a pattern is just a mess that you're always making.

From December 2020 to January 2021, Sam Riviere composed *Conflicted Copy* using Generative Pre-trained Transformer 2 (GPT-2). GPT-2, first released a little over five years ago, was a large language model trained on eight million web pages, capable of responding to prompts with text that it generated on the basis of knowing what normally happens next. GPT-2 was a mess. As anyone who played around with it in the months after its launch might remember, it could produce plausible prose given strict parameters, but it was quickly liable to either become repetitive or veer off topic. The effect was a little like talking to a new friend in the smoking area as you're coming up: an initial rush, followed by the regular euphorics, ending in well-meaning incomprehension. For a spell, a bug 'flipped the sign of the reward' in its code, which meant that it began to churn out, as its creators OpenAI put it, 'not gibberish but maximally bad output'.[1]

Unlike the more advanced chatbots – cured of erring – which we are now lumped with, this meant that GPT-2 was fun. It existed somewhere in that space between aleatory freedom and the patterns that make such freedom bearable. Riviere doesn't anywhere elaborate on how he used GPT-2 to put the poems together, but the results rock between the voice of a doltish salesman ('The current print and PDF set may sell faster / so you might prefer to get this one now' ['9']), flavourless doses of self-help ('What / you really want might not be exactly the / same as things you really enjoy doing' ['16']), and sudden spasms of genuine weirdness: 'Then another

---

[1] https://openai.com/index/fine-tuning-gpt-2/

guy tried making light of the occasion using / what appeared to be old footage of Nazi leaders shooting / captured pigeons during World War II' ('41'). Although the jacket tells us the poems have been 'stripped of the usual authorial clutter', the best of them often read as a quixotic dialogue between a disillusioned dreamer and his upbeat sidekick:

> Now you're done with
> the usual paper and ink
> (unless this sounds like
> a bad idea), you're free to
> wander out of the study
> room into the open air ('5')

Thank you, GPT-2. The bot gets entertainingly snarky when it reflects on its own incapacity to wander anywhere, a fact that crops up now and then to unsteady the otherwise collaborative spirit:

>   the poet
> himself has never been capable, despite
> repeated efforts and promises, of actually
> giving me the body I am dreaming of. ('23')

The dream of a (bodiless) language without 'authorial clutter' has probably now been realised with subsequent iterations of ChatGPT. It is a boring dream. I read the first half of the collection in a hair salon with AI-generated lo-fi cloying along in the background – the Uriah Heep of noise, so sycophantically inoffensive that it picks holes in your sanity. Nothing is allowed to fall out of place when a machine takes the next move from the aggregate of all next moves ever taken. The interminable reproduction of what has been runs on the logic of predictable connections: link after link, step by step, the necessity of what follows is assured. What we get is 'maximally good output', which is to say the worst conditions for creating art yet imagined.

On the face of it, Riviere is dabbling with the wizardry of our promised future's sleek connectivity, communing with the utopia that's coming at us with its rictus smile and its glazed-over eyes which can't see past the certainties of yesterday. It's a future in which, with a few taps, we will all be able to read the book we think we want to read, and save ourselves the trouble of encountering how other people think and want in the meantime. But because GPT-2 was, as I've mentioned, just a little rough around the edges, it could still allow for the 'rare kind of error' ('17'), as one poem put it, which reveals language to be a living substance, one that is laced with all the mistakes and flaws, as well as the less interesting perfections, of its users.

This means that *Conflicted Copy* might be better read not as an early adventure in AI–human collaborations but rather as the latest, and just maybe one of the last, mystical efforts to write conjunctively and chaotically (rather than connectively and predictively) with found material. The idea that language is one measureless Ouija-board putting us in touch with a hidden truth that can only be rationed out in the broken parts of our sad and clumsy syllabling is probably as old as language itself. In the twentieth century, automatic writing, free association, Stein's 'composition as explanation' and Dada's *découpé* all owed something to this vision. The motivating assumption here, applied with various degrees of rigour and self-consciousness, was that language is always doing more than we know, and certainly more than we can ever expect to control or predict.

Conjunction and disjunction, not connection and disconnection, are better ways of describing how this works. Syntax is, of course, about fitting the pieces together in a recognisable order, but in doing so it rubs together non-semantic elements of language in such a way that sparks start flying. Saying anything at all means saying more than you want to say. Language uses us in unforeseeable ways, and whenever we forget this, we're a little less alive than we might otherwise be. In a 1965 talk on his concept of poetic dictation, Jack Spicer puts it like this:

> But what you want to say – the business of the wanting coming from Outside, like it wants five dollars being ten dollars, that kind of want – is the real thing, the thing that you didn't want to say in terms of your own ego, in terms of your image, in terms of your life, in terms of everything.
> And how this operates, I haven't the vaguest notion. You could probably figure it out scientifically if you knew enough about the science of chance, combination, permutation, all of that. I don't know. But I know that it has happened.[2]

In the techno-utopia (forever coming right up), Spicer's edgy 'Outside' of language will be replaced with an AI built on large language model learning. It will impeccably connect the next sentence to the last. It will render the mess as pattern – as though really, finally the interference of human whim and error could be contained. Thankfully, language is too apt to surprise us, precisely because, like Spicer suggests, before it arrives at any one of us, it has spent a long time passing through all the whims and errors that precede us. This is Riviere's collaborator GTP-2, working hard to describe what it is about language that exceeds the scientific calculations that have made its own existence possible:

> Even today you are an
> outsider in your own mind, an observer whose
> existence is a reflection of that other presence,
> like another star, or something trapped inside a
> closed room, that forces it to manifest and
> evolve in unpredictable ways – all without
> ever revealing its inner nature. ('30')

Poetry is good at trapping language in closed rooms, and so forcing it to evolve in unpredictable ways. Riviere shows us how, for a brief while, poetry shared this talent with an AI in its adolescence. I'm not sure they'll have so much to say to each other in the years to come. Then again, who knows.

---

2 https://writing.upenn.edu/~afilreis/88v/spicer-dictation.html

A Tool To Preserve Presence

Lily Petch, *From Stone to Clay to Butter* (Dunlin Press) £9

Reviewed by Anthony Barnett

Discovering captivating early poems scattered throughout painter Celia Paul's memoir *Self-Portrait* (Cape, 2019) has set me to thinking about artists who also write poems. This is nothing new: from centuries ago Michelangelo's *Sonnets* easily comes to mind, in several translations, including that by Elizabeth Jennings (Carcanet, 2003). *Some Poems* by Paul Klee was nicely put into English by Anselm Hollo (Scorpion, 1962). Picasso too, who liked to put his hand to most everything. And doubtless, Celia Paul does not see herself as a poet on an equal footing as an artist, but some certainly do, David Jones, Blake, equally or even more so. Three whose work I have become most recently acquainted with are Monica Ferrando: her painting and philosophy essay, with Giorgio Agamben, translated from Italian, *The Unspeakable Girl: The Myth and Mystery of Kore* (Seagull, 2014), is her only book in English, though Barry Schwabsky has translated a suite of her poems, with drawings, in *Snow lit rev*; Lu Rose Cunningham, a graduate of Glasgow School of Art, who, amongst other, innovative work, makes wonderfully complex and thoughtful drawings – drawing is not a lost art for her (Cunningham's Broken Sleep poetry book *Interval: House, Lover, Slippages* is reviewed in *PNR* 270); and now Lily Petch, just graduated from the Slade with a material oriented installation for her degree show.

Dunlin Press, in Wivenhoe, is a publisher very much in favour of interactions between literature and art. In fact, Lily Petch's poetry debut *From Stone to Clay to Butter* is text only, but is to a large extent drawn from a brick-coloured cover book of texts, photos and diagrams ancient and modern, displayed in an open case of reclaimed bricks at her degree show, apropos, but not only so, the origin of language: *The written unit, signs, gravemarkers and the left behind object*. Petch's description is 'To pay close attention to the way in which we treat writing as a tool to preserve presence beyond the boundaries of the body. A tribute to the act of recording traces of ancestry by sign.'

In *From Stone to Clay to Butter*: 'Thoughts surrounding the invention of the written unit – born from a categorisation of surrounding objects and entities.' And 'First there was this large thing which bore a kind of substance you could eat': that's tree and fruit. I do not think I can do justice quoting just a line or two: 'The below surface feels infinite'. Petch's writing is filled with knowledge, wisdom, discovery, mysteriousness, and it is, I believe, in defiance of a kind of matter-of-factness, magical and beautiful. This is most lovingly, even if heart-rendingly, embodied in a new poem Petch has written entitled 'But What Is Forward Now All Is Dust', from a three-poem sequence, 'Daybreak', which shadows motifs already to be found in *From Stone to Clay to Butter*:

> And the wind said, 'try seeing the whole of history
>   so far unravel itself'.
> So we harnessed a tool and a sign and a tongue and
>   shot our way off
> into the future.
>
> And she said in reply, 'after destruction the forward
>   motion to
> reparation must be warped – the linear path must
>   be altered'.
> So we broke it apart beneath our feet until the tool,
>   sign, and tongue
> could no longer grasp its meaning.
>
> And after all this the soil said, 'skin on skin is best'.
> So we buried the broken fragments of some kind of
>   meaning where skin
> could find no touch to linger.
>
> ('But what is forward now all is dust?')

Longing for Lost Rivers

Eliana Hernández-Pachón, *The Brush / La Mata*, translated by Robin Myers (Archipelago Books) $17

Javier Peñalosa M.: *What Comes Back / Los que regresan*, translated by Robin Myers (Copper Canyon Press) $18

Reviewed by Chris Miller

Wozu Dichter, when something is rotten in the state? 'The aesthetic principle of stylisation [makes] an unthinkable fate appear to have had some meaning... This alone does an injustice to the victims; yet no art that tried to evade them could confront the claims of justice': Adorno, natch. The two books reviewed here attempt a kind of reckoning with their respective states, Colombia and Mexico.

Hernández-Pachón's *The Brush* concerns a massacre (16–22 February 2000) perpetrated by the AUC, a far-right paramilitary terrorist group formed by landowners in opposition to the Marxist guerillas of the Colombian civil war. (The AUC is thought to have killed nearly 100,000 Colombians over the course of its history.) The victims in this case were the villagers of El Salado, some 200 of them. The Marine Corps battalion responsible for the area was mysteriously withdrawn. The AUC, like other terrorist groups, were *narcotraficantes* and the massacre was conducted with maximum cruelty: chainsaws were used, those not yet killed were forced to witness the killings, there was rape and torture. The incident was investigated, there are reports: what can poetry add?

Hernández-Pachón answers this question in interview: 'there are things that poetry can do better: working with ellipses, for instance, and evoking what can't be named'. Her book justifies this faith. It is tripartite: in the first two parts, we hear of Pablo and of Ester (a couple) – fictional archetypes, one of whom survives; their life in an isolated house is given a novelistic particularity. The third part is given to the Brush/la Mata as it and the Investigators and the Witnesses speak.

Hernández-Pachón conducts her memorial like a Greek tragedy. Everything occurs offstage, with the la Mata as a kind of chorus: as the poet says, 'human temporalities aren't the same as nature's'. Her named protagonists and la Mata speak in verse. The text requires meticulous reading. Ester's escape is obliquely registered: 'Better to keep walking / And if her legs protest / forget her body altogether'. Are the villagers hiding? Yes: 'a foot thrust in the air: a raised leg takes a step'. To emerge is death: Ester wishes she could say 'I don't even think of hunger anymore'. La Mata records the slow absorption of the deserted village by exuberant fertility (in the Colombian edition, María Isabel Rueda's illustrations gradually absorb the pages). The Investigators tabulate trajectories ('The air's resistance slows its flight. Even so, the bullet entered through the right side') and count bullets, as though effacing death by their objectivity: 'Seventy more of these bullets are fired that day. A mere ten strike the trees.' The Witnesses compare the AUC to the irresistible invasion of night. This combination of localist realism (Pablo and Ester) with something more like mythology in the voice of la Mata casts a new light on the events. The peasants are mystified, passive, stoic and mostly dead: 'Yes, we heard something, but we said nothing...'; 'It's always better not to know'. They tentatively correct the Investigators. At the end, women begin to return to the village. Domestic tasks again become central to the day. The women are celebrated as light and as flowers, and for 'the love that rises from them like a coral reef'. They are less permanent than la Mata but more persistent than the almost random invaders, who shot and tortured to the sound of amplified music or the beat of drums. A postface by Héctor Abad asks how horror should be narrated, citing Celan, Primo Levi and Truman Capote. Hernández-Pachón's patchwork of genres, a kind of generic polyphony, can live with this company.

Javier Peñalosa M. evokes the state of the Mexican nation in almost medieval fashion; here is an allegorical progress, in which the 'pilgrims', mostly anonymous, advance through a shifting symbolic landscape. The medium is rhythmic prose. At the heart of that landscape is the quest for water; *What Comes Back* is suffused with longing for the lost rivers – many now riverbed paths – that are three-times listed, the second time under the ironic Nahuatl name, 'close to water' (Anáhuac). Ecopoetics is thus added to the substantial ambitions of this volume. Each page requires new forms of interpretation. Ornithomancy is a constant but predictably evasive presence. Do we hear alchemical symbolism in 'These were the days of the Great Works. They called the cavity *construction*. / Out there, a group of men was making the next century's ruins'? – or a mockery of Mitterandian ambition? The pilgrims pass through Genesis, a recreation of the world (though water is still absent), and an Edenic phase: 'I felt like I could call the trees by their names'. Then we seem to be in Trakl's 'Ein Winterabend', with 'The table is probably set, he said'; now we have a foot in the Heraclitean river; the stones of the riverbed have become a graveyard; there is the menace of those 'gathering in the darkness... they had light but were using it to blind'. The 'pilgrims' fall from Edenic grace: '... we were abandoned at dawn by what we'd thought was evident'. Evil gains traction: 'None of us knew where to find the red-stained ones, the brusque-skulled. / And one of our own said mournfully: We opened a door. We left it open all night long.' But there is compassion, too, for these blood-stained men: 'They're thirsty too, she said. And they're someone's aching heart.' Rationality seems to dissolve the firmament and 'the temple.' Prodigies occur. Shamans intervene. A Mary-Celeste house is found, in which a child is now only the record of his growth marked on a wall. There are rumours of eco-disaster in coastal saltmarshes. Now the pilgrims seem to be blind and discordant: 'We are the words [Logos] that will arrive' (*llegar*) turns into 'the words that will wound' (*llagar*). When they find water, it lacks the power of baptismal redemption. But there are words of hope: 'The water's body can't be buried, it always comes back, it doesn't know how to disappear'.

In the next section of the book, the protagonists are named in each poem's title, but here the prose has become hopelessly vague: 'The sign of her house was invisibility. She would move her body about, leaving blank spaces among the furniture.' (The translation is not at fault, though the purpose construction in the second sentence has – understandably – gone missing.) Are these monuments to imaginary *desaparecidos?*

In the last section, something like a human sacrifice seems intended to revive a watercourse; an aqueduct has been blocked, as if the marvels of the Aztec past were similarly occluded; a double murder or suicide follows, and water (I think) returns, at first as mud; the female victim is ultimately buried in a *zanja* (irrigation ditch). The feminine object pronoun here could be victim or water, and the confusion seems deliberate.

This chaotic summary might make *Los que regresan* sound like an obstacle course; in fact, a part of the book's rather haunting charm is its unassuming language (poet and translator can be heard reading this section on the Archipelago website):

> At dawn, a line of light appeared in the distance.
> It wasn't the first, but this light was different for us.
>   As in the old books, it sundered what was united
>   in darkness and gradually revealed its shapes. It
>   separated above from below.
> And we couldn't see the water, but something
>   fluttered on its surface.
> The great firmament above and us below.
> The inverse of the water above and us below

But the book is marred by its excessive ambition; the price of Peñalosa M.'s polyvalency is a certain lack of focus. Certainly, its relevance to the hideous gang-regency of the cities bordering the USA is remote at best. But perhaps this parallel with *La Mata* is irrelevant. *What Comes Back* is a plangent allegorical quest, a political *via negativa*, and, as such, less informative than Montale's brusque negatives: 'This, today is all we can tell you: what we are *not*, what we do *not* want' (Galassi's translation). It is a kind of state-of-the-nation poem, full of beautifully realised symbols, but the poet 'cannot' – to this ear – 'make it cohere'.

By contrast, Hernández-Pachón has achieved something substantial by her very indirection. She is not a native or descendant of the area around the Montes de María, with its unique habitat, and had to research its flora for the poem. At a recent reading, the inclusion of *frailejones* (Espletia grandiflora) was questioned by a Colombian anthropologist, since it is native to the páramo, and the poet confessed that it was simply a plant that she particularly loved. The technical difficulties thus presented to the translator are obvious, and Robin Myers has risen to the occasion with grace and ingenuity. I thought she was in error about *pastilla* (water-melon rather than clementine?) but she had, in both these cases, the privilege of working with the poets, both of them English speakers; Hernández-Pachón, a Columbia academic, is presumably close to bilingual.

In interview, Myers talks of translation decisions as 'always and only that: a decision that could have been otherwise' – here, for example, the decision to favour brevity over the plural in the title of *Los que regresan*. That is correct, but does little justice to the authority with which she, as poet and translator, leads her readers through the difficulties of these two texts. My local quarrels over detail come from one constantly looking from the Spanish to her English for guidance. In particular, the stylistic variety of *La Mata*, which goes from the splendidly colloquial thought or utterance of Pablo and Ester to the febrile Churrigueresco of la Mata's own voice, interspersed with the procedural language of the Investigators and the obstinately inarticulate voices of the victims (behind which trauma hides), has been masterfully conveyed. Myers is a prolific translator of contemporary Hispano-American poetry and novels, and usually acquainted with those she translates.

Talking of *La Mata* in a recent piece for the Poetry Society of America, Myers turned for a parallel to the Israeli massacres in Gaza – and American complicity in them. It is, of course, Western demand for drugs, combined with the Western war on drugs, that form the context of *La Mata*, along with the United States' traditional support for fascistic, racist governments in the Americas. The little sense I have of *narco* savagery is gleaned not from experience but from that very literal medium, film – for Mexico, for example, from the films of Amat Escalante, in which outrage at blind inhumanity cries at intolerable volume. Poetry should not forget politics, even as it erects a graceful and apophatic monument to the victims.

An Infinity Gone

Ian Patterson, *Collected Poems* (Broken Sleep Books) £17.99

Reviewed by Jack Barron

Seriousness needn't be heavy. Indeed, T.S. Eliot saw the way to Tennyson's heart through a critical mode that kept things light: 'By looking innocently at the surface we are most likely to come to the depths, to the abyss of sorrow'. Of course, true innocence can't know this, and only knows itself in being lost, and Eliot, *faux-naïf*, thereby takes on the misdirectional air of a whistling pickpocket. But nonetheless the approach wisely marks out the complex intimacies a critic – and a poet – might find between the light-handed and the heavy-hearted. Skimming across the surface of Ian Patterson's *Collected Poems*, things are similarly innocent-looking: 'So to Speak', 'Prattle', 'This and That', 'Quite Right', 'Easy to Say', 'No Way', 'Small Change', *Bound To Be*, 'Nothing Doing', 'What Ever Next?'. Such phrases bear the unassuming nonchalance of small talk. Taken into the pressurised atmosphere of verse, however, their breezy speaking sounds a sudden, sorrowful depth: *Bound To Be* describes a phatic existentialism; 'Nothing Doing' gives a Heideggerian impetus to absence; 'No Way' is theatrical disbelief and a genuine dead-end. These small gestures of nothing, then, are not, in Patterson's hands, for nothing: they are the forms of speech – at first glance so innocent – that pass most unthinkingly between us and, in doing so, utter the hidden worlds in which we always are.

Therein abstraction meets humanity: 'a bit open, that floating tired light seemed to fade the people / gone, an infinity gone, touches of life curving off some other way' ('Cold Again'). The infinite is beyond any of us, but 'an infinity', more softly spoken, with worldly indefiniteness, brings the eternal home: it is those minor acts of living, themselves immeasurable, that, in the end, touch us most keenly. In the same way, 'in some other way' studies its own vagueness, tested against the human contact that vocalic encounter – whether a conversation or a poem – needs, and the result of which none can predict. And such a fine sensitivity is at PLAY right through this significant body of work, a most precise attentiveness paid to all these endless nothings that 'sustains us on the edge of talk, grey / absent or annulled, to the core / streaming out loud across the entire space'. For twenty years, Patterson taught English at Queens' College, Cambridge, and the specially receptive atmosphere of his verse is indebted to his critical forebears, to I.A. Richards and William Empson: a way of reading, and writing, in which any and all linguistic exchange will sing for the justly attentive ear.

But Patterson is also able to swerve the potential bourgeoise clever-cleverness of the New Critical classroom, and therein acknowledge the political life of words, through a persistent interest in the European avant-garde. Across his oeuvre, we find various traces of Surrealism's dreamy re-seeings: 'lemon fills my eyes with tears' ('Pencil'); the streetwise romance of John James: 'diminishing as I pass, doing and undoing / like ash settling' ('Still Visible'); as well as the academically deranged language-games of late Prynne: 'A flag of light turned actual rupture, a scrap of art noted / till I rest, watch stopped' ('Something in the Air'). But, as we can see, for Patterson, there remains a great sense of an 'I', however deferred: a lyric presence speaks – to you – through and with the syntactic chaos, and his poems thereby arch recurringly from the singular to our collective polity and, in doing so, create a pathway for the strange creature, caught just outside of subjectivity, that goes some way to define each of us.

A poetics of this unique kind is, it turns out, prize-worthy. In 2017 Patterson won the Forward Prize for Best Single Poem for 'Plenty of Nothing', first published in *PNR* 230. An elegy for his wife, the writer Jenny Diski, the poem is as impossible and commonplace as death is:

End a hard time to get enough pink forms to reconcile
    two worlds of the mind to say the least and work
safe hands on what we know to move abroad like
    autumn

Comprising eighty-four almost-unpunctuated lines, a reader must choose their own moments of pause, or else become breathless. In this, the poem necessitates active resistance to its plenitude by the spaces it demands; one's being becomes entangled with the poem's, and some hard-won understanding is achieved: 'to say the least' is to say it all when speaking of a life spent together. In the innocent-looking domesticities – 'pink forms', a promise to 'move abroad', 'work' – is the teeming plenty of nothing, the sorrowful abysses that occupy so much of our time, and, at *that* time, mean – seemingly – so little: 'The hoover fades beneath the lethal march off this page'. The poem offers no conclusion, apart from absence twinned with endlessness: another finitude come, another infinity gone. Nothing lasts forever.

What To Do When You Can Do Nothing?

Sasha Dugdale, *The Strongbox* (Carcanet) £12.99

Maria Stepanova, translated by Sasha Dugdale, *Holy Winter 20/21* (Bloodaxe) £12

Reviewed by Rebecca Hurst

Sasha Dugdale's latest collection, *The Strongbox,* and her translation of Maria Stepanova's collection *Holy Winter 20/21* were both published in 2024. The two books stepped into the world hand-in-hand, and their reckoning with war, pandemic, ecological crisis and displacement are gut-wrenchingly pertinent.

For the past few months I've written, unwritten and rewritten this review, as the world seems to unravel faster than my brain can comprehend. In 1988 my history teacher told us with gloomy confidence that the Soviet Union would last another 100 years. A couple of years earlier, radioactive clouds from Chernobyl had drifted over my Sussex village. I've never believed I live outside the stream of history, but with every year that passes I feel more forcibly its turbulent currents. Writing has become difficult; reading too, intermittently.

> Must we write a poem
> about this, o Muse? How
> do we even begin?

writes the Ukrainian poet Oksana Maksymchuk in her debut collection *Still City* (Carcanet, 2024). Silence is one option, but an option that feels akin to defeat; and maybe not an option after all as Stepanova suggests:

> And what to do when you can do nothing?
> We sing and we sweat, both bodily functions.

Some books you tumble into, like falling headfirst down a well; an immersive experience. This is *The Strongbox*, from its opening sequence, 'Anatomy of an Abduction' – and the story, set in motion by the Fates, of a young girl, groomed online and convinced to leave her home and travel to a warzone:

> It began with the sun
> appearing over the plane wing
> supernatural orange
>   but no light
>
> A night of bitter memories
> sitting bolt upright
> phrase book on her lap
> travelling east

Other books walk alongside you more coolly ('How fish cling fast-bound in the ice, their mouths again / And there is no one to free them. Nor understand me'), until a moment when the poems reach out and wring your heart. This is *Holy Winter 20/21*:

> Blow winds. A crowd of unknown ghosts.
> I sing heartbroken, alone and old, I sing
> To myself. The rags of fog hang
> In the twilight. A flurry of snow
> The wind whistles. My glass of wine
> Is gone, the bottle empty.
> The fire dwindles in the hearth.
> Whoever speaks, speaks in a whisper.
> I think about how these letters mean nothing.

Writing a book of poetry that reckons with war, pandemic, ecological crisis and displacement – who will hear you? And yet as Stepanova concedes, speaking in or through one of many translated and borrowed voices that are heard in this collection, somehow the writing goes on:

> The winds were icy, I made conversation with them –
> After all I had nobody else – and then the cold suddenly spoke:
> 'Still writing the poems, old fool? Well keep writing, if you must?'

Perhaps because by writing a book of poetry you ensure that the people who read you will *really* read you. They will absorb your words by that slow, osmosis-like process poetry demands of its readers. Joni Mitchell said the trouble with poetry is that reckoning with it is like getting the meat out of a sunflower seed. But I've ridden on Russian trams where the floor was crunchy with a deep litter of sunflower seed shells.

Hermes appears towards the end of *The Strongbox*, cold and alone on the frontline of a war, as miserable as Auden's centurion. In a time where much of what is put into words is done so with indecent haste, manicured to appeal to the algorithm's search engines, refined and polished by AI – where the sunflower seeds are empty husks yet we continue to break and bloody our nails on them – a collection of poems can matter deeply because what it contains is painstakingly considered. Each word and punctuation mark matters and has been reckoned with. There is comfort in a slowness of reading that mirrors the care, attention and time spent composing. Time that is doubled when the collection is translated, when 'the translation calls to the original within'¹. As the exiled Stepanova (via Ovid, via Dugdale) writes:

> I'm old but I keep going, grey, but I'm still at it
> As if it wasn't my poems that got me holed up in the Far North
> ...
> As if literature was indeed the most vital of all the arts

And a little later, writing of bunkmates in an icy barrack in words that summon the closeness of the translator and their source, and of these two poets who 'have different voices singing the same tune'²:

> You and me drink from the same mess tin
> At night we lick each other's souls...

What else to read in the age of Trump and climate crisis and a world slouching its way towards fascism? In the Soviet Union Boris Pasternak wrote of a candle burning on a table in a land given over to a snowy blizzard. Now, in *The Strongbox*, we read of a different kind of burning, where:

> In the dirty fire of the great poets
> there are lines of such naturalness
> that when you have torched the source
> you too must end in wordlessness.

Yet Dugdale's book ends not with wordlessness, but with the image of a compromised man lifting a lyre. How else to make sense of our fragile humanity – stranded, as Stepanova describes, in one of the circles of Dante's inferno – than to travel through language to a place where:

> There are no walls, no roof
> Only the Northern Lights
> And a few shared histories
> Opened anew, like little doors.

---

1 Walter Benjamin, *The Translator's Task*
2 From: *'I sometimes wonder why I translate. It expands something in you': Translator Sasha Dugdale. An interview on translating from Russian, poetry, and publishing.* Anita Gopalan, 2 September 2021.

Some Contributors

Andrew Dickinson is a literary critic and medical student. His monograph, *Elizabeth Bishop and the Styles of Writing*, is under review with Cambridge University Press.

Andrew Shanks is a retired Anglican priest; once Canon Theologian at Manchester Cathedral; author of scholarly works including, in 2024, *Apocalyptic Patience: Mystical Theology / Gnosticism / Ethical Phenomenology*; and *Sublime Virtue: 'Sainthood', as Rendered Problematic by a Dozen Novelists*.

Anthony Barnett's new mashup of poetry and prose is *My God, You Have a Lot to Answer For, But You Won't, Will You: Sing Songs* (Allardyce, 2025). He co-edits *Snow lit rev*.

Dan Burt's last poetry collection was *Salvage at Twilight*, 2019, and last chapbook *A History*, 2022. His memoir, *Every Wrong Direction*, was published in the UK and US in 2022. He is a lawyer, investment banker, businessman and Honorary Fellow of St. John's College, Cambridge.

Gail McConnell is a poet and critic from Belfast, currently editing Ciaran Carson's essays for Gallery Press.

Gregory Woods's most recent collection was *Records of an Incitement to Silence* (Carcanet, 2021). His booklet, *They Exchange Glances: Gay Modernist Poems in Translation*, is published by Hercules Editions.

Harry Sanderson teaches undergraduates at Newnham College, Cambridge.

Jack Barron grew up in the north-east of England. He now teaches English at the University of Cambridge. His work, critical and poetic, has appeared in *Textual Practice*, *The London Magazine*, *PN Review*, *Shearsman Magazine* and elsewhere. He was shortlisted for the 2024 Observer/Anthony Burgess Prize for Arts Journalism.

Jena Schmitt lives in Sault Ste. Marie, Ontario, Canada, with her children. Her poetry, short fiction, essays and drawings have appeared in journals in the UK, Canada and the US. She is currently working on essays about the writers Claire Malroux and Ingeborg Bachmann.

Laura Scott's first collection, *So Many Rooms,* was published by Carcanet and won the Seamus Heaney Prize in 2020. Her second collection, *The Fourth Sister,* came out in 2023.

Rebecca Hurst is a Manchester-based writer and opera-maker. She is the author of a poetry collection, *The Iron Bridge* (Carcanet), and a poetry pamphlet, *The Fox's Wedding* (The Emma Press).

Sujata Bhatt has published nine collections of poetry with Carcanet Press. She has received numerous awards. Her work has been widely anthologized and has been translated into more than twenty languages.

Tara Bergin has published three collections of poetry with Carcanet Press, most recently *Savage Tales,* which was one of the *Irish Times* 'best new poetry books of 2022' and winner of the Michael Hartnett Poetry Award 2024.

WWWW.PNREVIEW.CO.UK

Editors
Michael Schmidt
John McAuliffe

Editorial Manager
Andrew Latimer

Contributing Editors
Anthony Vahni Capildeo
Sasha Dugdale
Will Harris

Copyeditor
Maren Meinhardt

Designed by
Andrew Latimer

Editorial address
The Editors at the address on the right. Manuscripts cannot be returned unless accompanied by a stamped addressed envelope or international reply coupon.

Trade distributors
Combined Book Services Ltd

Represented by
Compass IPS Ltd

Copyright
© 2025 Poetry Nation Review
All rights reserved
ISBN 978-1-80017-471-9
ISBN 0144-7076

Subscriptions—6 issues
 INDIVIDUAL–print and digital: £45; abroad £65
 INSTITUTIONS–print only: £140; abroad £162
 INSTITUTIONS–digital only: from Exact Editions (https://shop.exacteditions.com/gb/pn-review) to: PN Review, Main Library, University of Manchester, Oxford Road, Manchester, M13 9PP, UK

Subscriptions & Enquiries:
support@pnreview.co.uk

Supported by